TABLE OF CONTENTS

In loving memory of my mother
Mona Jacqueline Beaman

THE
Whole
Truth

How I *Naturally* Reclaimed My Health And You Can Too

Andrea Beaman
HHC, AADP

Copyright© 2005 by Andrea Beaman, HHC, AADP
www.AndreaBeaman.com
email: Andrea@AndreaBeaman.com

Published by Andrea Beaman, New York City

All rights reserved. No part of this book may be reproduced in any form
without permission in writing from the publisher, except by a reviewer
who may quote brief passages.

This book is not intended as a substitute for medical advice from a physician.
The material contained in *The Whole Truth – How I Naturally Reclaimed My Health
and You Can Too*, is for general information and the purpose of educating
individuals on nutrition, lifestyle, health & fitness and related topics. Should you
have any health care related questions, please consult with your physician or
other qualified health care provider before embarking on a new treatment, diet,
fitness or exercise program. You should never disregard medical advice or delay
in seeking it because of something you have read In *The Whole Truth – How I
Naturally Reclaimed My Health and You Can Too.*

Cover design Julie Mueller
jam graphics & design

FOREWORD

Medicine was originally established to be a source of health and healing, but in recent years has become a profit- driven industry. Big business and government have a pro-business model instead of a pro-health model when it comes to health-care.

Americans deserve an effective, efficient system based on prevention, holistic health education, sound nutrition theory and high-quality personal care.

As the founder and director of Integrative Nutrition, I am committed to dramatically improving the healthcare system in America. I truly believe the way to achieve this goal is to educate and empower people who are passionate about healthy foods and lifestyle, and train them to work with the public.

The first step in creating this tremendous change is to look at the food we eat. The food we take into our mouths goes into our stomach where it gets digested and eventually assimilated into the bloodstream. Our blood is what creates our cells, our tissues, our organs, our skin, our hair, our brains and eventually, our thoughts and feelings. We are, at our most basic level, walking food.

Despite the confusing and often contradictory information that floods the world of nutrition and health, the basics are simple. Most people already know what they could or should do to improve their health. They will tell you they should drink less alcohol, increase exercise and eat more fruits and veggies. However, knowing what to do doesn't mean they are actually doing it.

What inspires me about Andrea Beaman is that she transitioned from the standard-american lifestyle - eating junk and being sick - to a new life of vibrant health, and a fulfilling career. She is a living, breathing example of how changing one's food changes one's life.

In this book, Andrea combines important facts about the current food and health industry with inspirational stories of personal triumph. She tackles the medical industry, the advertising industry and the controversial food subjects of dairy, meat and genetically modified foods. Woven into her story, Andrea highlights the importance of exercise, self-expression, emotions and spirituality. She explains how they, in addition to food, are essential forms of nourishment. These aspects of life determine the extent to which our lives are fulfilling, enjoyable and worthwhile.

I hope you enjoy reading Andrea's story and that it motivates you to examine your own level of health. You are the only person who can make yourself healthy. The first step is to slow down, listen to your body and understand yourself from the inside out. May this book help you in that journey and inspire you to live a fulfilling, healthy and long life.

joshua

Joshua Rosenthal, MScEd
Founder and Director
Institute For Integrative Nutrition
www.integrativenutrition.com

ACKNOWLEDGMENTS

I want to thank many people, but to do that would be an entire book in itself! First and foremost my mother: my eternal gratitude to the woman who carried my soul into this world, created my body in her own, and taught me how to love. If it were not for her life and death battle with breast cancer, I would not be where I am today – healthy, free from illness and teaching people how to do the same.

Thank you to all the great healers, teachers and philosophers throughout the ages – the information I learned from these wise souls had, and continues to have, a great impact on my learning. I utilized valuable information from each to create a healing plan that has worked masterfully on my own health and the health of clients too. A partial list of these "healers" who have come before me includes: George Ohsawa, Michio and Aveline Kushi, Naboru Muramoto, Christine Pirello, Paul Pitchford, Alex Jack, Steve Gagne, Elson Haas, Kristina Turner, William Dufty, Wayne Dyer, Deepak Chopra, Louise Hay, Marianne Williamson, Emmet Fox, Tich Nat Hahn, John Kabat Zinn, Joshua Rosenthal and the Institute for Integrative Nutrition, Julia Cameron, Jack Canfield, Bernie Siegel, Ralph Waldo Emerson, Henry David Thoreau, Hafiz, Jesus Christ, Gandhi, and countless others.

A multitude of thanks to *all* of my clients – you continually teach me significant insights about illness and how to truly heal the body, mind and soul. Thank you for having the courage to believe in the power to heal yourself. You inspire me to continue teaching people about the connection between better food and better health.

And, my family… thank you to my father, Richard Beaman, for teaching me to move forward no matter what, and to always question authority! If wasn't for those lessons and a whole lot more I would have been just another diseased statistic stuck in the health care (disease care) system. Thank you Erica for helping me finally kick candida out the door! And, for your amazing editing job - I couldn't have done this without you. Thank you Lyndon Swammy for the fantastic headshot photos on my website and books. Thank you Danny for creating the best smoothies ever! Thank you Marc and Donna for keeping me on my toes about health and encouraging me to make cooking videos. Thank you Marc Anthony for teaching me about what really matters in this world; fun, freedom and love. Thank you Andrew Beansquash for showing me how to really thank God for everything… including a doorknob! Thank you Brandon for experimenting with sea vegetables… but please stop eating the slimy ones you find washed up on the shore at the beach. Thank you Ricky for giving my brochure to everyone you meet. Thank you Imma G for filling up my cooking classes with lots of people who are hungry for healthy information and great food. Thank you Terry for trying to get votes for my video on the Food Network. Thank you Uncle Al for being sensitive and awake to non-violence and peace.

Thank you to my many wonderful friends and business associates who have loved and supported me in my dream of creating a healthier world. Thank you Kim Gantz for taking me out of my kitchen and encouraging me to get out into the world, and for your ongoing love and support. Thank you Elizabeth Konecky for eating well, getting pregnant, and blessing the world with Matan (the gift).

Thank you Dina Maiella-Marro, you are truly my Emerson and I love you! Thank you Super Dave Marro for my website – you did an amazing job and it's beautiful. Thank you Katharine McMaster for believing in me and loving me even when I eat too many darn chocolate covered almonds (organic, of course). Thank you Debra Bergman – our video is great. Thank you Barry Herstik for the delicious food pictures on my website. Thank you Howie Jacobson, Maureen Piper and John Mollenhauer. Thank you Joy Pierson and Bart Potenza (Candle Café), Benay Vynerib, Julie Austin, Linda Nealon (and Rose), Delia Quigley, Temple Tracey Brooks Seger, Robert Parker, Jeannie and Anthony DelGreco, and I'm sure I missed a few hundred folks. I feel truly blessed to know and love you all.

Many thanks to all the healthier food restaurants and markets in New York City and around the globe for making delicious food available for the masses.

And, last but not least, thank you God for the huge wake up call. I am grateful for my illness and recovery, and doing my best to wake up as many people as possible to a better way of living and eating.

INTRODUCTION

Sickness is a BIG business. And, the American consumers have unwittingly bought into it, perpetuating poor health. I learned this first-hand when my mother was diagnosed with breast cancer, and we utilized modern medical treatments (surgery, radiation and chemotherapy) as a "cure." The common allopathic medical procedure with cancer, or any disease for that matter, is to eliminate the symptoms. However, eliminating symptoms, whether they are tumors, aches and pains, runny nose, high blood pressure, constipation or indigestion, can never determine the root cause of the actual disease. Symptoms are the body's way of conveying a message to us that something we're doing isn't appropriate and we're creating an imbalance causing the body to malfunction. In modern medicine, by killing the messenger (the symptom), the question "what is contributing to, or causing this malady," is not addressed.

After treatment, the patient could return to specific diet and lifestyle habits that may have initially contributed to the sickness; high stress job, poor quality food, lack of physical exercise, absence of spiritual practice, etc. Eventually, new symptoms or the same disease reappears causing the patient to take more medication or suffer through an additional surgery. With this scenario being the case more often than not, it seems our health care system is "sick" and needs to be re-examined.

My mother's battle with breast cancer (twice) opened my mind to a deeper perspective of disease and its initial causes and possible cures. But, it wasn't until my own illness took root and grew that I made the diet and lifestyle improvements needed to heal myself.

I was diagnosed with thyroid disease. The doctors prescribed a lifetime of medication for me; according to their knowledge there was no direct cause or *cure* for my bodily dysfunction. I didn't believe that to be true, so I went against the doctor's recommendation and radically altered my diet instead of chaining myself to prescription drugs for the rest of my life. I stopped consuming junk food, fast food and diet food, and replaced it with *real* wholesome, seasonal, and organic meals.

The cure for my ailment didn't come after one meal, or after one month of meals, but became more evident with ongoing self-care. The more I consciously cared for myself with proper diet and exercise, the better my health became. Instead of spending thousands of dollars on drugs that couldn't offer me a cure, I wisely invested that money and created a true health care system that enhanced my well being on every level.

After healing my disease, I was perplexed as to how I had initially become so far removed from my body and it's capacity to self-heal. All creatures in the world know exactly what to eat to keep their body functioning optimally. It's innate. It's in everyone - including me, but somehow I had lost touch with that basic knowledge.

Being subjected to a lifetime of persuasive advertisements telling me what to eat and why, it was clear how someone could easily lose sight of their own ability to make the best choices. Furthermore, if a drug advertises that it can alleviate symptoms (headache, menstrual cramps,

6

congestion, nausea, etc.), once again the connection becomes lost as we dull the body's many signals for relief. An interesting advertising example; I grew up drinking diet soda and eating non-fat, low-fat, diet foods believing they would help me lose weight, but it wasn't necessarily true, and eventually those non-nutritive foods contributed to my malfunctioning body. As you continue reading you will discover that diet foods and artificial sweeteners are one of the worst foods for health, and can contribute to weight gain.

To reconnect with intuitive knowledge I had to figure out my physical and emotional needs. I researched food and its effect on health, and then experimented with that food in my own personal laboratory – my body. What I discovered went against almost everything taught in school, or suggested by any government agency promoting food (USDA, FDA, etc.).

Once I deciphered what my body and mind holistically needed to be able to thrive, I committed to integrating the best possible choices as often as I could for the sake of my health. Since then, my life and health have monumentally transformed. Today, I am living at my ideal weight without dieting, my health is excellent, immune system is strong, and my supposedly "incurable" thyroid disease is cured.

I've written *The Whole Truth – How I Naturally Reclaimed My Health and You Can Too* as an inspirational guide to help you understand some simple truths about health and natural healing. My ultimate goal is to empower you, the reader, to use what you learn in this book and apply it in your own life to help you achieve your ideal weight, vibrant health, and a full recovery using the practical philosophy of eating better quality food and incorporating simple lifestyle suggestions.

If you are one of the many people looking for a true cure because you are sick and tired of being sick and tired, or are just seeking better health, this is the right book for you. Interspersed throughout this book are healing, heartwarming, and eye opening stories of burgeoning health awareness, combined with hard facts about the energetic effects of naturals foods, the consequences of relying on medication, and how to tap into your body's self-healing ability to make outstanding health an everyday reality.

I am confident you will find many valuable insights within these pages to help you discover your own truth about how to reclaim your health, and look and feel your absolute best. Thank you for letting me give you The Whole Truth about my personal experience from sickness to wellness – and for the opportunity to teach you how you can do it too!

"The most satisfying thing in life is to have been able to give a large part of oneself to others." - Pierre Teilhard de Chardin

Wishing you vibrant health,
Andrea Beaman, HHC, AADP
Holistic Health Counselor
American Association of Drugless Practitioners

CHAPTER I

<u>AWAKENING THE TRUTH</u>

This book of health was borne out of sickness - my mother's battle with breast cancer and my own thyroid disease. These two events woke me up to some simple truths about the cause and cure of modern-day diseases, and were the catalysts that helped me transform my life, health and profession.

In 1980 my mother experienced a dull pain inside her armpit. The pain persisted for several months, and eventually settled into her breast where she discovered a small lump.

The doctors performed a battery of tests and a mammogram, but couldn't find anything serious. They told her the lump in her breast was non-cancerous, reassured her the dull pain was nothing to worry about and sent her home.

One year later, the lump grew larger and the dull pain had now become sharp. She returned to the doctors once again and this time was diagnosed with breast cancer. With great trust in modern medicine, she battled breast cancer with a radical mastectomy and chemotherapy.

The doctors did what they were trained to do, and they removed her breast, lymph nodes, as well as all of the tissue down to the bare bones of her rib-cage. They went to war on her body and eradicated the breast as if *it* were the cause of her cancer.

After she returned from the hospital, I asked her to show me how they *cured* her disease – I was a curious thirteen-year-old girl and needed to know. She led me into the bedroom and locked the door. She slowly undressed and showed me her wound. Her entire breast and all of the skin around it were removed and I could see the indented bones of her rib cage. The area from her armpit to the center of her chest was shiny, hard, pink scar tissue where soft flesh used to be. She showed me the places on her once fully freckled legs that now sported long whitish pink strips. She told me the skin from her legs was used as grafts, and applied to her chest to help it heal. I had never seen anything like it, except maybe in horror movies, but I knew one thing for sure - a radical mastectomy was certainly very radical.

After the surgery mom bought a soft, rubbery foam insert to put inside her bra to fill in the void. The fake breast was supposed to emulate a real one, but the detachable mass fell out of her bra every time she took it off. She confided in me that it was a constant reminder of what she didn't have anymore.

At the time, I didn't fully understand the extent of my mother's traumatic experience or how much she suffered from the removal of her body part in order to extend her life. I was just happy she was alive.

We returned to our "normal" lives and continued doing the things we always did without dramatically changing our diet or lifestyle. However, my father read something about the negative effects of caffeine on breast tissue, so her ritual morning coffee was no longer a part of her daily diet.

She continued to go for semi-annual check-ups and was assured that the cancer was no longer growing inside her body. Each day we grew

10

more confident about her health and after five years Mom was considered "cancer free." The surgery and treatments had worked and the offending breast with its disease had been successfully terminated.

In 1992, approximately eleven years after her mastectomy, she had a dizzy spell and fainted in the bathroom. Medical tests revealed the breast cancer had come back with a vengeance and spread throughout her entire body. She had cancer in her lungs. She had cancer in her brain. She had cancer in her liver. She had cancer in her bones. She had *breast* cancer everywhere… even though she no longer had the diseased breast.

Once again we utilized the recommended "cancer cures," radiation and chemotherapy, and attempted to poison the disease out of her body. I was older now, for this second coming of cancer, but still very confused about the process of curing it. Every week I drove her to the Long Island clinic for another dose of radiation on her head or some other body part. The technicians would lock her into a large metal container, and then leave the room and close the door behind them to ensure their own safety from the deadly rays of radiation.

Mom would emerge from the room feeling disoriented and exhausted. Every week we returned to the dreadful container, and every week she grew ever more frail. Instead of feeling healthier from these treatments she was feeling the detrimental side effects of radiation and chemotherapy poisoning. She was nauseated and couldn't eat. She slept all day and night with brief waking moments. She had frequent bouts of diarrhea and couldn't keep anything in her system. Her naturally soft, curly, red hair was thinning and falling out. The first to completely disappear were her eyebrows, and soon after that, all that remained on the top of her head was soft orange peach fuzz. Her sparkling green eyes lost their brilliance and became bloodshot and dull. She was dazed and had no energy. It seemed like she was barely alive at all.

With each harsh treatment her vibrancy and love of life waned. The perpetual smile that once lived on her face was lost as the life force drained from her in that harmful room of radiation. Within a few months she could no longer climb the stairs inside our house. We relocated her to the sofabed in the living room where she would live for the next year.

She didn't want to continue the treatments, but we kept taking her because it was the only way we knew, what we were told, and what we believed to be the cure. It was the accepted truth on how to *kill* cancer, recommended by the professionals in modern medicine and accepted by mainstream society.

Something wasn't right with this deadly process of battling cancer and I sensed it intuitively. We began experimenting with various healing alternatives from shark cartilage to lipids, to vitamin supplements like E, C, selenium, lecithin, beta carotene, co-enzyme Q10, spirulina, blue green algae, and many others therapies too. We expanded our minds and wanted to try everything we could.

While doing some research, my father read an article about a Dr. Hugh Faulkner who had cured himself of terminal pancreatic cancer by using something called a Macrobiotic Diet, so we decided to give it a try. It was only food, and it couldn't hurt Mom anymore than what we had already subjected her to.

We read various books about this macrobiotic diet that emphasized organically grown whole foods, grains, beans, vegetables, sea vegetables, fruits, nuts, seeds and small amounts of animal food (preferably fish).

Growing up as a mostly middle-class "Standard American" family, the macrobiotic diet was definitely a stretch from what we were eating. It was food in its whole form, and not packaged or highly processed. It didn't come out of a frozen dinner box and couldn't be quickly popped into the microwave. It wasn't heavily laden with chemicals, sugar or other addictive substances. And, it was organic which meant, "grown without chemicals and pesticides."

It took time and effort to prepare, and cooking it was inconvenient, but within a few weeks we witnessed a positive change in Mom's energy levels. We accepted this new diet as a possible healing option and decided she would travel to the Kushi Institute in Massachusetts and attend the Way To Health Program for one week. Mom was too weak to go alone so I went with her. Dad drove us from Queens, New York, and dropped us off in Beckett, Massachusetts, for our re-education of food and its connection to health.

The natural health practitioners believed that changing the quality of food could change the quality of our blood and, in effect, change all the cells in the body, eventually curing the illness. They spoke of healing naturally from the inside out.

The concept sounded interesting, unlike anything I'd heard before. Something about the sheer simplicity of it resonated deeply within me and made complete sense. I questioned the conventional medical path we had taken with Mom and had a strong feeling the harsh chemicals put inside her body had a detrimental effect, rather than a healthy one. She was not separate from her cancer, and I concluded those same chemicals administered to destroy the disease, were destroying her too. After all, the

13

human body is made up of mostly water, and very few things can survive in a polluted lake full of chemicals and radioactive waste.

Within forty-eight hours of arriving at the Kushi Institute and ingesting this "foreign" food, three meals a day, I felt a difference in my body. For the first time in my life, my bowels were moving on a daily basis. This was the first sign of what I believed to be a positive physical change.

The second thing I noticed was I required less sleep, but had more energy. It was strange because I wasn't consuming the foods that would normally increase my energy like coffee, soda, or sugary snacks. I learned that using stimulants like sugar and caffeine to artificially increase my energy would make me more tired, and in need of more stimulants. Regardless of the Macrobiotic practitioners teachings, I certainly couldn't deny the physical effects I felt inside my own body.

At the end of the week, I walked downstairs into the living room at the main house and found mom lying on the couch, with her head propped up, reading a book. I couldn't believe it! She walked down the stairs, without assistance, and was alert, awake, and reading! She looked up from behind the book and smiled at me.

It had been a long time since I'd seen her beautiful, loving smile. Her freckled face had a peachy color, and the pink tone of her lips was returning from the grayish, pale color they had been one week prior. Her green eyes sparkled with life and she giggled when she saw me staring at her with my jaw agape. I took her ability to laugh as a sure sign of regenerating health.

After one week of experiencing the effect of this natural diet on myself and witnessing the transformation in mom, my own truth about

14

curing illness began to change. We left the institute renewed with hope and went home to try and recreate a similar healing experience by cooking healthy food, reading books instead of watching television, and incorporating daily exercise.

At home she was still very weak, but now had some extra energy to get out of bed occasionally and cook some macrobiotic meals with me. We also walked to the park two or three times and exercised lightly. The future looked brighter, but Mom was still exhausted and slept a lot.

A couple of months later, in May 1993, I was scheduled to graduate from Nassau Community College and she wanted to attend the ceremony. As I helped her get dressed, she caught a glimpse of her naked body in the full-length mirror. She stopped me from dressing her and stared at her reflection. Her eyes welled with tears and she said, "Ann, I look like I'm a concentration camp victim."

I couldn't argue with her. Her legs looked like bones with a loose covering of skin attached, and she weighed less than eighty pounds. Her eyes were sunken and dull. Her face was gaunt and pale, and no hair had yet grown back on her head except for a small coating of peach fuzz. She still had the remnants of radiation sickness and chemotherapy poisoning.

When she first began losing her curly red hair we bought a wig for her. She wore it only once or twice and then retired it because she didn't like the way it looked on her - it didn't look natural. It sat on top of the television attached to the Styrofoam head that lived beneath it.

Standing before the full-length mirror on graduation day, I continued dressing her while she cried. Instead of putting on the unflattering wig I wrapped a soft, colorful, green, red and tan scarf around her head. She looked again at her reflection, smiled and said, "Ann, now I look like a gypsy." She tried to maintain a smile, but I could see she was sad. She said she didn't recognize the person staring back at her in the mirror.

At the graduation ceremony I walked up to the stage, grabbed my diploma and headed back down the aisle to my seat. I looked over at the bench where Mom was sitting with Dad. She was hunched over. It seemed like the weight of her head and upper body was too heavy for her to hold up. She slowly lifted her head and looked at me as I passed. She smiled her loving smile, the one I remember being so simple and sweet it made her eyes look like they were twinkling.

I was happy she was there that day and I was proud of her too. She was my mom and I didn't care that she didn't have any hair on her head or any eyebrows either. I didn't care that she was pale and thin. I didn't care that she had a disease. I only cared that she was still alive.

After graduation, our new "healthier" way of eating and living wasn't fully intact and we eventually slipped back into watching television all day long and not exercising. We tried to eat the best we could, what we learned at the institute, but Mom's energy continued to wane. She was still in a severely depleted state from the war that was waged on her cancer and just didn't have the physical strength to fully reclaim her health. It was difficult to watch.

I would cook for her, clean her, shower her, and dress her on a daily basis – I was her full-time nurse, and she was my best friend. Eventually, we had to hire a live-in Macrobiotic Cook to help with some of the cooking responsibilities.

Mom and I would lie in bed and watch talk shows for most of the day, and she would always cry for the guests and their sorrowful life experiences. I would hand her a box of tissues and poke fun at her for being so sensitive. It amazed me that she could weep for people she didn't know, especially while she was having terrible troubles of her own.

In November 1993, a year and a half after her second diagnosis of breast cancer, suddenly her breathing became labored and heavy. One evening we were lying in bed watching television and she weakly asked me for a Sarsaparilla.

I laughed and said, "A sarsaparilla? What on earth is a sarsaparilla?"

"It's a root beer."

"A root beer?" I had read about the detrimental effects of sugar on cancer and I refused to give her a root beer soda.

She begged, "Please Ann, just one little sip."

I told her it wasn't good for her and would make her even sicker. In my arrogance, with my newly enlightened mind, I thought food was the only panacea that could *cure* or *kill* her. After all, I believed her eating habits had set the stage for cancer to arrive in the first place and that I was doing the right thing by denying her simple request.

She repeated, "Just a sip, Ann."

"Stop bothering me about it," I yelled.

Her eyes welled with tears and she turned her face away so I wouldn't see her cry. She waited a brief moment and then asked me once more for one little sip of sarsaparilla.

I was annoyed with her insistence at asking for the same thing over and over again, and I was frustrated, and tired, and scared of losing her, and angry that she wasn't healing at fast as I hoped she would. I wanted to shake the sickness out of her and hold her until she was well again, but I

17

didn't, and I couldn't. Instead, I completely lost control of myself, and my senses, and I cursed at her and I blamed her for not getting better, and then I stormed out of the room.

If I would've known on that day in November that a root beer soda would be the last thing she would ever ask me for, I would have dug up the sarsaparilla root myself and ground it with my bare hands, adding to it as much refined white sugar as needed to make it the sweetest drink she ever tasted in her entire life. And then, I would have spoon-fed her every last drop of it until she was completely satisfied.

Three days later on November 12th, 1993, mom returned her soul back to her creator, and we returned her frail, war-torn body back to the earth.

Truly, I was blessed to be able to share her life and death experience with her. She was an amazing human being who taught me great lessons about love, compassion, life, and health, especially in her time of dying. I only wish we would have had more time.

After traveling down that path with my mom, I vowed if ever I was diagnosed with something serious I would seek an alternative, health-promoting solution first and a conventional medical solution last. That life-altering event awakened in me a larger truth about how to be healthy, but I wasn't ready to fully to live it yet. Within a short amount of time after my mom's death, I foolishly returned to my old habits of junk food, fast food, sugar and stimulants, and it wasn't long before my own sickness manifested four years later.

CHAPTER II

TRANSFORMATION AND RECOVERY

Although my intuition strongly urged me to eat better quality food, soon after my mother's death I reverted back to my destructive lifestyle habits. I had no desire to take full responsibility for my health, and incorporate the basic self-care needed to help disease-proof my body. I *was* dysfunctionally programmed and waited for the sickness to come and get me before I made any effort to change my ways.

I didn't have to wait long before an illness took root inside me and was nourished by my poor food choices. Four years after my mom's death, at age twenty-eight, I made a doctor's appointment because of recurrent illnesses. My immune system was a wreck and I had frequent flus, colds, and unsightly cold sores. My cholesterol was well over 200. I was anemic, weak, lethargic, and about twenty pounds over my ideal weight. I had recurring bouts with depression, and my energy was chaotic and imbalanced. I was either up really high, or down really low, but rarely ever feeling centered or healthy. I felt miserable, and looked like crap. Especially with a blistering cold sore on my lip every other week!

The doctor took blood tests and informed me I had hypothyroidism, and it was the main cause of my many ailments. The conventional medical cure suggested was to take radioactive iodine to terminate my malfunctioning thyroid, and then take a prescription medication called synthroid (synthetic thyroid hormone) for the rest of my life.

Sounding eerily familiar, red flags went up! I did *not* want to destroy any part of my body with radiation and then be chained to a drug for the rest of my life. As a witness to the dreadful effects of radiation on my mother's body, the thought of taking radioactive iodine, or radioactive *anything,* repulsed me.

I remember after my mom died, my brother Terry gave me a book, "World Without Cancer," by G. Edward Griffin. In this eye-opening book, the author discovered that radiation and chemotherapy were both initially tested on concentration camp victims in Nazi Germany to establish how much the human body could withstand before expiring.

I had no desire to expire!

The similarity between what a cancer patient looks like and what a concentration camp victim looked like was undeniable. My mom saw it, too. She made the connection when she looked at her own emaciated image in the mirror. I believe that every time another person is deliberately exposed to radiation or chemotherapy, the Nazi's intention of destroying human beings has survived the war.

I informed the doctor I would *not* take the conventional medical route, but was going to heal my thyroid using natural foods instead. The doctor told me it was "impossible," and the thyroid could *not* be healed through changing the diet.

I knew she was just confirming what she had been taught by modern medicine about healing the thyroid… or more appropriately, what she hadn't been taught. I stood firm in my decision because I wanted to heal my body, not harm it, and believed I was better off with all of my body parts intact to be able to achieve the goal. Giving my body proper fuel and energy to heal itself, instead of damaging it, resonated deeply inside me as the way to reclaim my health.

Without a second thought, I traveled to the Macrobiotic Summer Conference in Vermont and had a health consultation with a Japanese man named Michio Kushi – a pioneer in the "natural foods" movement. He did something during my check up that no doctor had ever done before… he took a long, studious look at me from head to toe. He examined my skin tone and texture, my eyes, face, tongue, body shape, hair, toenails, fingernails, and then gave me his educated assessment.

He shook his head back and forth and said, "Eating too much dairy, frozen dairy especially, and stimulants, and sugar."

I couldn't believe it! He was right on the mark. The main staples of my diet at that time were pizza, frozen yogurt, coffee and sugar, sugar, sugar. It was as if he had x-ray vision and could see what was going on inside my body by looking at the outside of it.

He touched my enlarged neck where my thyroid was and told me that I could heal it within four months, but then patted me on the arm and said, "If you don't change your diet right now, full blown breast cancer in both breasts within five years."

I immediately thought about my mom and knew he was right about my diagnosis. Every month during my menstrual cycle I would experience sharp pain in my breasts, and it would take many doses of Midol (at least 10-12 pills) to alleviate the symptoms.

Michio told me he saw a discoloration on my body that indicated the beginning stages of breast cancer. He said, "the beginning stages," because cancer doesn't happen overnight. He explained that no one wakes up one day and suddenly has cancer. It takes many years, growing undetected, before it's substantial enough to be diagnosed by modern technology.

At the time of my diagnosis, a day in the life of Andrea Beaman consisted of two cups of coffee with nutrasweet and skim milk, and a bagel with nothing on it to start the day, a slice of pizza for lunch, fat-free frozen yogurt as a snack, pretzels, jellybeans, chocolate and other candy, and of course, more coffee in the afternoon because I needed the caffeine to help me make it through the day. I was a nutritionally deficient, fast food and junk food junkie, and I was feeding my body a steady disease-promoting diet.

When my wake-up call came, I answered it, and was ready to make the necessary changes to transform my health. I *had* to! If I didn't I would be enlisted in the same deadly war as my mom, and I had no desire to let modern medicine go to battle on my body.

I returned home from the Macrobiotic Summer Conference and radically altered my diet to the recommended whole grains (brown rice, quinoa, millet, barley, oats and others), all types of beans, a wide variety of vegetables with an emphasis on dark leafy greens, sea vegetables, fish, nuts, seeds, and seasonal fruits.

Within fourteen days of committing to my new eating regimen my body began to discharge, what looked like, toxic waste! I woke up every morning and coughed up large clumps of white, sticky phlegm. What was releasing from my body was gross, but I kept moving forward because I physically felt myself changing on the inside.

Four weeks after transitioning my diet my face glowed with renewed health and vitality. I had no facial blemishes, and none of those nasty cold sores popped up to ruin my life. My eyes were bright and alert and my energy levels surged and remained constant without the use of coffee or stimulants. I was growing more confident that this new way of eating was having a positive effect on my body.

During that healing time I ate the largest portions of food than I ever had in my life. At breakfast I'd take leftover grain from dinner the night before and cook it into a soft porridge by adding water and heating it for a few minutes. I'd also add some crunchy toasted walnuts or almonds, sunflower seeds, sweet raisins, and rice or almond milk to make it creamy and delicious. My lunch usually consisted of a large portion of leftover dinner plus a bean soup or miso soup. And, dinner was my biggest meal of the day: brown rice or some other whole grain, beans, sautéed vegetables, salad, a sea vegetable dish, soup and sometimes a piece of fish. Plus I ate healthy snacks two or three times per day that included fruits, nuts, seeds, vegetables, and hummus (chickpea dip) with whole grain pitas. And, with all that food I actually dropped twelve pounds in the first month! I was feeding my body a steady stream of better quality food, instead of starving it by restricting or limiting my intake to lose weight.

My clothes started to hang off me, and people noticed. One of the girls at work told me that although I looked "really good, and lost a lot of weight," she thought I should go back to the "old" way I was eating because she was afraid this new food was going to kill me! And, of course, she missed our afternoon ritual of going to Starbucks for Iced Latte's and then out for non-fat frozen yogurt with M&M's or Reese's Peanut Butter Cups on top.

Most of the people I worked with periodically stopped by my desk and ogled the "strange" food I was eating (rice and beans and vegetables!).

They said they couldn't stand its sight or smell, and for the sake of my health and theirs, I should return to the way I was eating before: bagels, candy and coffee. They wanted me to be "normal" again.

No matter what anyone said, I persevered and did what I knew was best to reclaim my health. Instead of listening to the external voices of some of the "unhealthy" people I knew, I got in touch with my internal voice, my body, and listened to what *it* was saying. I had more energy, regular bowel movements, and I physically looked better than I had in years. I lost weight without dieting or reducing my food intake, but had changed the *quality* and type of food. I stayed focused and broke free from old disease promoting eating patterns that were literally killing me!

After four months I returned to the doctor for another blood test, and the results showed my thyroid hormones had changed too! The doctor now warned that although the thyroid hormone had changed dramatically from where it was, it was still malfunctioning. She said my disease was not yet cured.

My thyroid continued to change for the next two years. It went from hypothyroid to hyperthyroid, and one doctor informed me I had Hashimoto's disease (another thyroid dysfunction). Every doctor I visited recommended prescription medication to heal my condition, and every time I declined the medicine. I changed doctors three times in search of someone that would offer another option besides drugs. I intuitively felt that my body would eventually find a healthy state and if I were to chemically intervene during that process it would have hindered my body's ability to heal itself.

Eventually, I stopped seeing doctors altogether because I felt they couldn't offer me much in the way of healing besides the medication I refused to take. So, I kept cooking and eating, and cooking and eating, for two years straight. And, I felt better and better with every wholesome, delicious nutrient rich meal.

Beyond food, I got the feeling I needed to use other healing tools to completely transform from sickness to wellness. I had spent a lifetime abusing myself with food, drugs, alcohol, negative thoughts, and many other self-destructive habits, and realized my body and mind also needed internal peace to heal. I had to create a self-loving space within myself, and incorporate spiritual and emotional work outside of the kitchen and inside my heart and mind.

I introduced meditation into my life to help calm my racing thoughts. I also practiced daily acts of forgiveness because I needed to forgive those who had hurt me in the past, and those I had hurt too. There were many old wounds inside me; the most painful was cursing at my mother on her deathbed. It weighed heavily on my heart and I needed to forgive myself.

I researched healing modalities from ancient cultures and exercised both physically and emotionally to clear stagnation from my body and mind. Daily physical activities like yoga from India and tai-chi from China became rituals for me. Becoming conscious of metaphysical (mind/body) connection to my illness enabled me to help change my *thoughts* and *ideas* about my inner self and the world outside me. And, before long, I had become one of those weird, crunchy, "new age" people I used to make fun of! Some of these healing practices will be covered in greater depth in Chapter VII – Satisfying the Senses.

Finally, for a complete healing transformation, I allowed my true voice to be heard. Interestingly, the area where I had my physical sickness (thyroid/throat) was where my voice lived. I had stifled my innermost thoughts, ideas and views of life for many years and needed to give myself freedom of speech. A great part of that emancipation included teaching other people how to naturally reclaim their health.

I committed to my health and consistently gave my body the energetic fuel (food), and other tools (emotional and spiritual work) it needed to heal. It took a little over two years for that health-promoting regimen to work, but it eventually did. Vibrant health didn't happen overnight, just as sickness didn't happen overnight either. It took time for my body to become unhealthy, and it took time, patience, work, love, and devotion to myself, to be able to fully reclaim my health.

When it comes to successful, long-term healing, I've discovered there are no quick fixes. I made the effort, did the work, and saw amazing results. And, if I can do it, you can do it too!

I am no longer dysfunctionally programmed and waiting for sickness to come and get me – I disease proof my body on a daily basis with the choices I make regarding food, exercise and spiritual practice. When my body feels off balance, instead of opting to purchase cold and flu medication, aspirin or prescription drugs to *cover up* my symptoms, I listen to my body and give it what it needs to truly heal.

Symptoms are a sign that something isn't right inside my body. In modern society symptoms are covered up with medications, ensuring worse sicknesses will inevitably manifest. Understanding this concept changed my life monumentally.

I've discovered that sickness is a BIG business and I wasn't buying into it on any level. And, to reclaim your health, neither should you.

CHAPTER III

<u>SICKNESS IS BIG BUSINESS</u>

A simple truth I needed to comprehend to retain my reclaimed health is that modern societies are built on business – and sickness makes up a significant portion of this business. Billions (make that trillions!) of dollars are spent every year on pharmaceutical drugs, surgeries, doctor's visits, and hospital care. One consequence: a segment of our population— easily numbered in the millions— is hooked on pharmaceutical drugs and not getting healthier, but are more sick and in need of more medications with each passing year.

It would seem that our healthcare system is not currently designed to promote lasting health. If it were, it would surely put itself out of business! I had one client who shared a particularly priceless insight with me. She had tried to have a baby, but was unsuccessful and decided to seek an alternative solution instead. When she came to me for a health consultation, I assessed her body was starving for proper nutrition and couldn't possibly create a life in such a severely deficient state.

Within a few months of overhauling her diet from highly refined, processed foods and too much dairy products, to a more wholesome diet of whole foods, grains, beans, vegetables, nuts, seeds, fish and small amounts of other animal foods, she became pregnant and had a beautiful baby boy.

While having a conversation with her about health, I shared my long-term goal of wanting to teach millions of people how to naturally heal themselves, beginning with altering their food choices.

She said, "If you succeed in teaching people how to heal themselves, you'll also succeed in putting yourself out of business!"

Luckily, my goal is much bigger than just keeping myself in business.

The thought of millions of people actually discovering the root cause of their illness, healing themselves, and feeling better in their physical (and emotional) self, is a beautiful goal to work towards. In terms of long-term *effects,* this does not seem to be the goal of our current health care industry.

One of the roles of the modern doctor is to remove an annoying symptom, and make the patient feel better temporarily by prescribing a medication. Treatment of this kind, over time, will eventually create deeper and more serious illnesses, and of course generate *more business.* This is called "treating a symptom" and will *never* get to the root cause of the problem to cure it.

If I experience pain in my body and take aspirin to dull it, I'm actually covering up the symptom of something else that's happening inside. The body is brilliant and will inform me of everything that's going on internally, if I listen to it's many signals. Any initial discomfort I feel is a warning that something is not right in my internal environment and deadening the pain with a medication will certainly not fix the problem.

A great example of "not listening" to a warning signal can be observed with the tonsils. When the tonsils become irritated and inflamed, it's a red flag hoisted from the immune system communicating that something is *not* right inside the body. Removing the tonsils is akin to killing the messenger! Once the messenger has been silenced, a whole host of other illnesses can begin to take root. Eventually, the body will need more serious attention, medication, or the removal of another organ as a result of this missed signal.

When I was seven years old, I had a traumatic accident and needed eleven stitches to close a wound across the bridge of my nose. After the surgery, I remember sitting in the hospital bed with white gauze taped across my face, listening to the doctor advising my mom to consider removing my tonsils. He asked me to open my mouth so they could get a look inside, and then he showed her my irritated, enlarged tonsils, and handed me a mirror so I could see them too. I thought they looked like big, red poisonous mushroom caps sprouting from the inside of my throat!

He asked if I had frequent colds, and throat infections. Both my mom and I told him my throat was constantly swollen; I lost my voice often, and was frequently sick. He suggested that while I was in the hospital he could quickly remove the tonsils and reassured us I wouldn't be as sick in the future.

The doctor was condemning my *tonsils* for creating the many maladies I was already experiencing in my young life. In truth, the poor food choices I reached out for had caused my poor health. At the age of seven I was already a full-blown sugar junkie, constantly compromising my immune system with the sweet, nutrient-depleting substance. Pop Tarts, Captain Crunch and candy were my main staples – sugar, sugar, and more sugar! My irritated tonsils were loudly advising me to "stop!"

The good doctor was a smart businessman. When you take your car in to get a tire fixed, the smart mechanic would check the oil, transmission and brake fluid, and then, for an additional fee, offer to change those too. That's exactly what happened to me while I was in the shop (the hospital), the physician checked under my hood and saw I needed other work too.

Removing an organ or body part is a costly procedure, and it can never be a *cure* for any disease. The body part itself is not the cause of the dysfunction. Hearts do not cause heart attacks, brains do not cause strokes, breasts do not cause cancer, and tonsils do not cause tonsillitis. The causes and effects of disease are entirely different. Modern day thinking about what disease is, what causes it, and how to cure it, is awry and prohibits true healing.

Taking a prescription medication cannot *cure* anything either, but millions of people are swallowing panaceas expecting miracles. When they temporarily feel better (because their symptom has been masked) they think the medicine worked. But there are no quick fixes to create a strong healthy body. Like anything else in life, it requires time, patience, and hard work to achieve important, life-enhancing goals.

All pharmaceutical drugs have detrimental side effects that can include: headaches, nausea, blurry vision, depression, psychosis, insomnia, liver disease, internal bleeding, low or high blood pressure, sexual dysfunction and impotence, digestive disorders, constipation, heart palpitations, and other serious ailments that will eventually require additional drugs or surgery to alleviate the newest symptoms.

An August 2003 research article in *Better Nutrition* stated, "Previous estimates suggested that nearly 5 percent of all hospital admissions – more than 1 million per year – are the result of (prescription) drug side effects."

30

Even the *side effects* of prescription drugs have generated billions of dollars! The medical industry is one of our most profitable, and the pharmaceutical industry is an integral part of that business plan.

For years, the medical establishment prescribed Hormone Replacement Therapy (HRT) for women experiencing the symptoms of menopause. It's been discovered that HRT's increase the risk of reproductive cancers, heart attacks, strokes and blood clots. These potentially fatal "side effects" are hardly worth masking the symptoms of a natural bodily transition that can be alleviated by making simple dietetic and lifestyle changes.

Whenever a drug is taken to alleviate a symptom, it will inevitably create an imbalance elsewhere in the body. Ultimately, the user will need another medication or major surgery to counteract the new malady provoked by this imbalance.

For example, men taking the prescription drug Viagra to increase their sexual potency have the potential side effect of blindness or a heart attack—a grave attribute for this popular drug. But, dangerous side effects are just one of the problems: not getting to the root cause of sexual impotence and other illnesses can be much more hazardous to overall long-term health.

Though prescription medications can make the symptoms disappear, the original problem will continually progress as long as it isn't properly addressed, resulting in a more threatening condition later. A quick look into an elderly person's medicine cabinet provides a clear picture of what happens when we rely on medication for "pseudo cures." It is not unheard of for an elderly person (sometimes visiting multiple doctors) to take twenty, thirty, or more prescriptions every day, and none of them work towards a cure.

Each new drug covers up the initial malady, allowing it to develop into secondary and tertiary conditions that will eventually require surgery, radiation, or other costly procedure. Prescription medicine will not get to the root cause of the problem, and it's not designed to. It's a band-aid, not a system for long-term wellness. As a result, the medical establishment and pharmaceutical companies make billions of dollars from the patient's inability to properly care for their self. These businesses use to make money from me too, but now I put my hard earned dollars elsewhere – into strengthening my health and disease proofing my body by making better lifestyle and diet choices.

I don't suggest abandoning the health care system, or to stop using the parts of it that *do* work. Trust me, if I experience a traumatic accident or break a bone, I absolutely want a doctor to put me back together again. I certainly don't want to be wrapped in seaweed and chopsticks and then left out in the sun to dry! Stitches, resetting broken bones, or anything traumatic that happens to the body requires professional medical services. This is where doctors excel. As far as sickness goes… pumping the body full of chemicals, resulting in the possible removal of a body part is not a method of "healing." Why pollute or dismember the body unnecessarily?

In ancient China, the doctor was paid only if the family remained healthy under his care and guidance. His job included teaching the patients how to *prevent* disease by altering their diet, exercise, and spiritual practice. If a family member were to become sick, the doctor was fired for not doing his job. Imagine that!

From my own perspective, I would schedule a visit to the doctor *after* sickness appeared. Using my health insurance *after* the onset of an illness means that it should really be called "sickness insurance." Paying into my insurance plan and not taking care of myself set up a future fund for an eventual ailment—which is exactly what happened. I know today that the only true health insurance is preventing disease from occurring in the first place.

I encourage clients to take an active role in their healing process, to listen to their body and decipher what it's saying. The body is constantly sending us messages that we have been taught to disregard. The little aches and pains, daily headaches, depression, frequent colds and flus, painful menstrual cycles, leaky bladders, prostate pain, and constipation, all have deeper meaning. The body will not malfunction or ache without a valid reason.

Running to the doctor for medication at the onset of each new illness weakens the body's ability to heal itself, and gradually creates a co-dependant relationship between doctor and patient, similar to that of drug dealer and addict. The patient numbs out and grows increasingly removed from their body, so that when a rash of bad headaches or constipation appears, they have no idea why and must rush to the doctor to explain their body's signals.

My old disempowering belief that I couldn't heal myself of an illness was a self-fulfilling prophecy. The more profoundly I believed it, the less attention I paid to my body, and the more alienated I became from myself. The doctors covered up the symptoms for me, and the responsibility for my health was fully transferred.

The reality is that your doctor does not live inside your body, you do, and the further you are removed from it the sicker you will become. Giving up responsibility for health results in a dependency on doctors and drugs that can potentially harm the body and worsen underlying conditions. This blind dependency is great business for the pharmaceutical companies and the medical establishment, but destructive for overall health.

Anything ingested into the body can either heal it or harm it, and pharmaceutical drugs seem to be promoting more of the latter. What is provided for us naturally by the earth is better suited to nourish and heal the body than what is prepared in a laboratory. We may be living in big cities and removed from a more natural environment, but we are still a part of nature.

Today, when the first symptoms of illness appear, I adjust my diet, exercise or spiritual practice, to help move through the malady quickly and easily. Healing my many illnesses began when I decided to take *full* responsibility and make real changes in my life. By taking my health into my own hands, I could no longer blame anyone else for my ailments, nor could I buy into the misconception that common diseases are an ordinary part of the process of life. They're not.

I used to believe that heart disease, cancer, arthritis, diabetes and other degenerative diseases were a normal part of human existence. Today, the argument for that belief seems astoundingly flimsy. Sickness may be common, but it should never be considered normal. The physical human condition can be healthy, vibrant and energetic for an entire lifetime, but only if the individual accepts responsibility for keeping it that way. The body is a magnificent creation; when given the appropriate tools, it can heal itself more permanently than any drug or doctor can.

These simple truths about the business of sickness changed my viewpoints, and responsibility to my self is how I accessed to the real business of healing. I took the time to re-educate myself, listen intuitively, and reclaim my power to heal. It required effort, time, self-care and commitment, but a healthy, vibrant life is worth everything it takes.

Everyday the choice to connect to myself and take full responsibility for my health is there to be made, and it has to be made over and over again. It's not a short-term thing like a diet that I can fall on or off of... it's about making better choices every day for a lifetime of wellness. By doing this, besides experiencing remarkable changes in my own life, I have witnessed the health of clients and friends improve after they too, reconnected and applied a better way of eating and living.

The question I stumbled upon after healing myself was *how* on earth did I get so disconnected from my body in the first place? I certainly thought I *knew* what was good for me and what wasn't, but for a long time I continued to ingest the junk and not care for myself or consider the long-term effects of my actions.

I believe part of the reason was because my mind was bombarded with modern society's ideas regarding health. The food and health care industries are businesses, and every thriving business has great advertising. The best advertising doesn't seem like advertising at all—it seems like my own thoughts and beliefs. And, that can lead to big trouble!

CHAPTER IV
<u>THE UNTRUTH IN ADVERTISING</u>

While embarked on my journey to reclaim my health, I took a one-year sabbatical from all major media including television, radio, newspapers and magazines. This experiment made me acutely aware that I was consistently being bombarded by other people's voices informing me what I *needed* to do to improve my life and health... and most of it was simply untrue!

The Archbishop of Canterbury said, "I do not read advertisements. I would spend all my time wanting things." The truth is, I did want something and it was called vibrant health, but I wasn't going to find it in an advertisement.

The ubiquitous advertising noise is everywhere: on the train, on the bus, the television, in magazines and newspapers, on billboards, written in the sky, and everywhere else an empty space formerly lived. The ads told me what to eat, where to eat it, what to wear, where to buy it, what to think, how to live, why I should own a specific product, and if I already owned it... why I should own another. With that external racket going on it was difficult to hear what my own body and mind were saying. And, I needed to hear myself in order to heal myself.

Every successful business advertises to draw consumers and increase sales. That's good business. Some ads are so effective, entire countries buy products and services that aren't necessarily good for their population and certainly won't benefit health in any way. Advertisers, even one's promoting "healthy" products, aren't paid to make the consumer healthier; they are paid to make consumers feel they absolutely *must* have the product or service, even if they don't need it. That is their job and they are great at it! *My* job is to take exceptional care of my body and mind, listen to what they're saying, and figure out what's really good for me. And, if you are seeking to reclaim or retain your health, I highly suggest you make it your job too.

"Advertising is a valuable economic factor because it's the cheapest way of selling goods, particularly if the goods are worthless," stated novelist and social critic, Sinclair Lewis.

That profound statement became evident while I rode the subway observing an advertisement from a local New York City hospital. The ad urged women to get mammograms for the safety of their health and to *prevent* breast cancer. This is clearly an ad for a service that I believe is *worthless* and *harmful* to the health of women.

Detecting a lump does not *prevent* breast cancer. By the time a lump is detected by a mammogram it's already been growing inside the body for many years. *Prevention* lies in taking the steps to ensure the disease doesn't take root and sprout in the first place.

I also strongly believe annual or bi-annual mammograms are downright dangerous. Squashing the breast in a metal clamp, possibly damaging cells, and then adding radiation to that area, does NOT make sense or promote health in any way. And, if cancer is not already present in the breast, after undergoing many years of mammograms and radiation and breast squashing, in the same spot over and over again, my intuition says cancer *will* be there eventually. Like Sir Isaac Newton said, "For every action, there is an equal and opposite reaction."

One morning during a torrential thunderstorm, I hailed a cab and invited the woman standing beside me to share mine. It turned out to be one of the most memorable cab rides of my life and helped to solidify my "controversial" view about mammograms.

I discovered she was a doctor/scientist working on the genome project and I told her I was a health counselor and natural nutritionist. She was curious to know how I got into the field of alternative healing. I quickly shared my story of naturally healing my thyroid by changing my diet from junk foods and fast food to organically grown whole grains, beans, fish, vegetables and sea vegetables.

She didn't seem surprised at all and then matter-of-factly stated, "Of course your thyroid healed, you were eating seaweed and it's rich in iodine."

I said, "If you know that information why on earth would any doctor perform surgery to remove a thyroid or use drugs to destroy it, instead of telling the patient to eat some seaweed?"

"Medication and surgery are quick and easy, and work. Besides, who has time to cook or wants to change their diet?"

She was absolutely right! As a health counselor I know how resistant people can be to making diet and lifestyle changes, but the truth is the body needs good quality nutrients and energy to heal. And, an even bigger truth is the body *cannot* be *healed* by destroying or dismembering it.

She asked why I decided to use food as a healing option, and I told her about my mom's breast cancer and our experiment with Macrobiotics.

38

She sternly advised that I "absolutely must" go for a yearly mammogram, and to begin them as soon as possible because I had a direct relative with breast cancer.

I thanked her for the advice, but told her I would *not* be going for a mammogram… ever!

I said, "After what you just told me about *why* doctors operate on the thyroid, I'll pass on the breast squashing, radiation ritual, and continue doing exactly what I'm doing – preventing the illness by taking the best possible care of myself with proper diet and exercise."

She chastised me, "Don't be foolish, go for the mammogram. Breast cancer is in your *genes*."

I don't believe that to be true. In my family, my mother was the first one to be stricken with breast cancer. No other relatives had it. There was no link to anyone other than herself to this dreadful disease. Where, then, was the hereditary gene factor for my mother?

A great example of this misconception that "cancer is in your genes" can be found in Asian countries where breast cancer was virtually non-existent fifty years ago. Today, the breast cancer rate in Japan is growing rampant and catching up to the American rate.

According to Breast Cancer Source, "Japanese women are five times less likely to develop breast cancer than American women. However, Japanese immigrants to the USA have been shown to lose this advantage within one to two generations, assuming the same risk profile as American women. This observation suggests that environmental factors play a role in developing the disease. Figures from epidemiological studies also indicate that the risk advantage demonstrated by native Japanese women may be dissipating: with the incidence of breast cancer in

Japan doubling between 1960 and 1986. This change in the prevalence of the disease may reflect the increasing adoption of Western lifestyles in Japan over the last fifty years."[1]

To reclaim health, it's imperative to understand that one of the most notable Western lifestyle habits other countries have adopted in the past few decades is eating Americanized fast foods and junk foods. This information is critical to help determine a major contributing factor, and root cause for breast cancer and many other common diseases.

The American Cancer Society warns consumers to steer clear of fast food, french fries, cheeseburgers, pizza, ice cream, doughnuts and other sweets for the *safety* of their health[2]. The evidence is mounting that excessively ingesting these lethal junk foods encourages the growth of many diseases.

One of the greatest achievements in marketing unhealthy, disease-promoting products is advertising to children and hooking them while their young, creating brand loyalties that can last a lifetime.

I participated in a health expo at a school in Washington Heights, New York. The organizer asked me to speak to the children, ages ranging from eight to fourteen years old, about the connection between food and health. During the discussion, I asked the kids what they thought was the best drink for the human body.

Hands popped up in the room and they yelled, "Coke, Pepsi, Milk, Gatorade, Diet Pepsi, and Sprite."

I had my hands full!

---

[1] Source: Sondik EJ. Breast cancer trends: Incidence, mortality and survival. Cancer 1994: 74:995-999.
[2] American Cancer Society – The Complete Guide to Nutrition.

There was a young boy sitting at a table drinking a Diet Pepsi. His big brown eyes were lost inside his puffed up face. He was sweating profusely and his entire body looked like it was overstuffed, and about to burst! His extra large rear-end barely fit on the standard size school chair, and his arms were thicker than my thighs. This child was clearly obese at age ten.

I asked why he thought Diet Pepsi was the best drink for him.

"Because it will make me lose weight," he replied.

The other children sitting at the table nodded in agreement.

I remember thinking the exact same thing when I was perpetually dieting and stuck in an overweight condition. It was not uncommon for me to drink a six-pack of Diet Pepsi a day, and yet weight loss still eluded me. Instead of losing weight I gained frequent headaches, blurred vision and a host of other conditions brought on by ingesting the artificial sweetener Aspartame a.k.a Nutrasweet[3].

I questioned another young boy why he believed Sprite was the best drink and he replied, "Because Shaq drinks it."

"How do you know Shaq drinks it?"

"From watching television."

Young minds are vulnerable, impressionable, and easily influenced by what their favorite star is *paid* to sell to them. Diet Pepsi and Sprite are popular beverages, but are *not* the best liquids for the human body.

I asked the children if they eat junk food and every hand, about 200 or so, waved frantically in the air. I asked them to explain how junk food made them *feel*. Their answers surprised me. Many of the children

---

[3] http://www.aspartamekills.com/, http://www.sweetpoison.com/, http://www.mercola.com/article/aspartame/dangers.htm

cited stomach aches, headaches, nausea, exhaustion, sleepiness, anger, sickness, and one young girl raised her hand and said, "Junk food gives me cancer!"

I wondered if she had already been diagnosed with cancer at age eight - which is not an uncommon occurrence in our modern society.

These little human beings were aware of what was happening inside them and made the physical connection that what they put into their body had an effect. Unfortunately, they hadn't been taught to listen to the signs (pain, nausea, stomach ache, etc.) or *how* to alleviate the malady in a natural way. As long as our children are hooked into the media and advertising they will always think that they are supposed to consume junk food and fast food even if it doesn't physically make them feel good.

I asked the children what foods they thought were truly healthy for the body and the overwhelming majority said vegetables.

They shouted, "Broccoli, carrots, corn, potatoes, french fries, and ketchup!"

I laughed, "French fries and ketchup?"

Those kids were right! French fries and ketchup are derived from vegetables. And, by the number of obese children present for the lecture, those two highly sugared and fatty, vegetable junk foods probably made up a big portion of their daily diet.

Our children need to be properly educated about nutrition, and taught to listen to their body to insure a healthy future, instead of a lifetime plagued with afflictions.

The declining health of our nation as a whole suggests that it's time to figure out whether or not a product is truly good for us, or if it just looks good and tastes good artificially. Great packaging, lavish promotions, and celebrity spokespeople have successfully captivated the attention of consumers of all ages, but many of the products being sold may not promote health and wellness.

Hormone Replacement Therapy (HRT) is a blatant example of how advertising has negatively affected and ultimately harmed millions of people. HRT ads suggested to aging women that taking these drugs and increasing the female hormone in the body will make them feel young and feminine again, increase bone mass, reduce hot flashes, and reduce the risk of osteoporosis.

The universal truth is a woman's body naturally *reduces* estrogen production at a certain age because there's a valid reason for it. As a woman reaches menopause her body's physical capability of having a baby diminishes – it's a natural and normal process. Besides, how many women would want to have children beyond fifty or sixty years of age? The human body is a magnificent creation and knows exactly what it's doing. All we have to do is listen.

In a New York Times article revealing the dangerous side effects of taking HRTs (heart attack, stroke, cancer) one woman said, "I am afraid. If I was taking it for hot flashes, I would come right off. But what about osteoporosis?"[4]

She and millions of others like her have been brainwashed into believing that taking HRT is the best answer for them. What they may not know is there are many other alternative solutions to keeping the body and bones healthy and strong. Specific foods can gently cool down the body,

---

[4] The New York Times, National, "Many Taking Hormone Pills Now Face a Difficult Choice, July 17, 2003.

reduce hot flashes, strengthen the bones, and create vibrancy without compromising health in the process.

One menopausal client in her mid-fifties experienced bouts of insomnia and uncomfortable sweating through day and night. Within three weeks of changing her nutrient deficient diet she reduced her hot flashes and other symptoms *dramatically;* they became acceptable and manageable.

The makers of aspirin and other pain relievers have advertised, "You haven't got time for the pain," and "Get moving again, pain free." I'm going to suggest that if you, the consumer, haven't got time to address the pain right now while it's a slight headache, joint pain or other uncomfortable feeling, than you had better make time for the bigger disease that may be on its way in the future. It's time to *stop*, make time for the pain, and figure out the cause in the first place.

Most recently, the controversy surrounding the popular painkillers Vioxx and Celebrex, and the increased risk of heart attack (approximately one in 300 patients!) has made headlines across America. Due to public outcry, Vioxx was pulled off the market, and then re-approved by the FDA and put back on the market. Yikes…be careful! Just because something is approved by the FDA does NOT mean it's safe. "America" is a business too, and its government agencies may not act in the best interest of public health.

After transitioning my diet the menstrual pain I had experienced in both my breasts and uterus subsided and eventually ceased. I stopped taking painkillers and began to listen to my body. It wasn't easy at first, but I began to hear where I ached and needed attention.

As I got in touch with my internal self I noticed when I ovulated I would experience a sharp pain and cramping in my left ovary. The gynecologist couldn't find anything, but I had a strong feeling something was there, it was just too small to be detected… yet. It can take a long time for a disease to grow before it's physically large enough for modern technology to discover the problem.

I felt that pain in my ovary for three years after changing my diet, but I knew it was just a matter of time before my body would eventually resolve the problem, what ever it was, on its own.

One morning, I woke, nauseous with debilitating cramps on my left side where I had the ovulation pain. I spent the next two hours in the bathroom shivering with a cold sweat that covered my entire body. After a painful and draining release from my bowels (as if I had food poisoning), I was exhausted and crawled back into bed. I woke up an hour later feeling refreshed and energized as if I had taken three shots of espresso coffee! It's been over five years since that incident and I've never again felt pain in my ovary.

I consistently gave my body the proper fuel it needed, and eventually and naturally it released whatever was stagnating inside me: a possible cyst, tumor, or fibroid.

As a consumer I have many choices: to buy or not to buy, to feel or not to feel, to heal or not to heal. Today, I choose to *not* dull the pain, but listen very carefully to what my body is saying and then give it the time, proper food and whatever else it needs to heal. I'm giving my body true cures instead of band-aids.

I discovered the best way for me to achieve this vibrant level of health was to stop listening to advertising noise, and beliefs of the modern medical establishment, and make my body my own personal laboratory. My illness was a blessing: it informed me it was time to get to know the body I was living in or I wouldn't be living in it much longer!

CHAPTER V
<u>BODY OF EVIDENCE</u>

For a more complete healing, I needed to reconnect with myself and understand my physical body. Its physical structure would inform me what I should, and should NOT, be eating to obtain great health.

As a toothless, grinning baby, I was unable to eat food that needed to be chewed, but nature remedied the situation by filling my mother's breasts with a nutrient dense *liquid*. Mom was fully prepared to supply nourishment for me, and I, being all gums at the time, was strategically equipped to suckle food directly from her breast. Her milk was designed perfectly to meet her baby's needs. Unfortunately, I didn't get any of it! Not one little drop. I believe this is where many of my health problems began.

During breastfeeding the mother implants immune strengthening nutrients, colostrum, and beneficial bacteria, for optimum growth and resistance to disease into the baby. Mother's milk also creates a healthy layer of mucus inside the baby's body enabling it to blink, breathe, and move its bowels, among other important functions. Human breast milk is essential to the growth of human babies, but many infants, including myself, have been deprived of this life enhancing liquid nourishment.

During the last century, medical science and the makers of baby formula had convinced moms across America that their natural breast milk was inferior to man-made formulas created in laboratories. This act of human egotism caused immeasurable damage to millions of babies and compromised their health as adults. And, it really makes me angry!

According to a news story on CNN.com, Sony Riviera, M.D. states, "Science is discovering more nutrients, immunities, essential fats and proteins that can *only* be found in human milk." The article reports that human milk banks are on the rise because the "medical research suggests that human milk is far superior to both cow's milk and baby formulas."[5]

Medical research also confirms that formula-fed babies suffer from an increased occurrence of diabetes, obesity, weakened immune system, intestinal diseases like Crohns, Colitis, and Irritable Bowel Syndrome, allergies, malabsorption, **thyroid disease**, eczema, respiratory infections and asthma, acid reflux, SIDS (sudden infant death syndrome), and overall poor health, than their breast-fed siblings.[6]

I was one of the millions of unfortunate babies who had been given formula instead of mother's milk, and I can personally attest to being plagued with a weak immune system, overgrowth of bad bacteria in my intestines, **thyroid disease**, eczema, allergies and a multitude of other ailments.

Human milk banks are proving to be a "cure" for disease-ridden babies and believe it or not, a prescription from a doctor is needed to have access to this magical substance. I've actually contemplated getting a prescription of mother's milk, but I think I'd be turned down due to age discrimination!

---

[5] http://archives.cnn.com/1999/HEALTH/women/12/23/breast.milk.angles.wmd/
[6] University of Washington Medical Research Center

Serious illnesses can occur early in life because the human baby is *not* designed to drink cow's milk, soymilk, or any other milk than that which naturally flows from its mother. The milk from each particular species is the perfect food for that species. The milk from the human breast is food for the baby human. The milk from the gorilla is food for the baby gorilla. The milk from the *cow* is food for the baby *cow*. Humans have chosen the cow, goat and sheep as our udders of choice, but these are no more fit for daily human consumption than is dog milk, cat milk or badger milk.

A baby is meant to drink milk from *its* mother and that's the bottom line. This is a universal truth and shouldn't be tampered with otherwise poor physical health is inevitable for both child *and* mother.

The mother is intended by nature to produce food for the baby and *not* releasing milk from her breast can cause stagnation and illness. Numerous studies have shown that women who breast-feed their babies are less likely to develop breast cancer.[7] My mother had five children, all of whom she didn't breast-feed. This, in conjunction with a nutrient poor diet, could have been one of the causes of her breast cancer.

Beyond the breast-feeding stage, the design of the body speaks again. As the baby begins to grow and form teeth, it should naturally begin to be weaned and given soft food. Mammals stop producing the enzyme lactase (used to digest lactose or milk sugar) and lose the ability to digest their *baby* food (milk) shortly after teeth are created. Ask any woman that has breast-fed her child and she can explain why the baby

---

[7] http://imaginis.com/breasthealth/news/news2.02.01.asp,
http://www.lalecheleague.org/NB/NBJulAug01p124.html,
http://www.lactationconnection.com/questions.htm
http://www.breastfeeding.com/all_about/all_about_more.html

should be off the nipple at a certain age. Contrary to what some adult men may believe… teeth chewing on the nipple HURTS! A good rule of thumb to remember: if there are *adult* teeth in your mouth, it's time to get off the nipple!

Most lactose intolerance is a *normal* condition and indicates the baby was properly weaned from its mother, but advertisements have adults convinced there's something wrong with their body because they cannot digest milk or other dairy products. Milk is baby food designed specifically for the growing infant. If the adult body is physically rejecting it, this is a normal process in the evolution of growth. Putting milk into our system after receiving signals that it's no longer advantageous, can eventually lead to disease.

According to a study in the Journal of the National Cancer Institute, "Dairy food may be the most potent factor in the development of breast cancer."[6]

Prior to changing my diet, I was addicted to the creamy white stuff and ate it every day in the form of pizza, frozen yogurt, ice cream, butter, coffee lattes, milk, cheese, and more. Taking baby food into my adult body created a baby-like body: pudgy, soft, with little muscle tone. I thought eating **non-fat** yogurt, **low-fat** cheese and **skim** milk was better for me and would help me lose weight. I was brainwashed by the "diet" and the "dairy" industry to think that was the truth.

I had been subjected to a lifetime of milk advertisements, and trained in a school system that used the Standard American Diet Pyramid as the guideline for my daily meals. I falsely believed, "milk does a body

---

[6] Paolo Toniolo, "Calorie-Providing Nutrients and Risk of Breast Cancer, Journal of the National Cancer Institute 81:278086, 1989. Let Food Be Thy Medicine, Alex Jack, One Peaceful World, 1999, p. 79.

good." Today, I know better. Baby food is *not* essential to my adult health and can be detrimental to my full-grown adult body when eaten in excess. I was eating dairy products at every meal, every day, three hundred and sixty-five days a year - that certainly falls into the category of "excess!"

Dairy is baby food and needs to be viewed as such, but I also believe it has positive attributes, too. Specific cultured dairy can benefit health, especially after undergoing rounds of chemotherapy or antibiotics that destroy internal mucus and beneficial intestinal flora. After chemotherapy, it's a good idea to take on a surrogate mother (goat, sheep, cow) to help bring the body back to a regenerative and properly functioning state.

Naturally produced, organic, hormone and antibiotic free yogurt and kefir are partially digested from the culturing/fermenting process, and can be easier to digest than most other milk products. If used medicinally, these products can coat the intestines with a layer of mucus enabling colonies of beneficial bacteria to attach and thrive. Without good bacteria in the digestive tract, absorption of food is limited and can hinder the healing process.

When clients come for health consultations I suggest they eliminate dairy products for a specific period and they usually become distressed by the mere thought of it. I believe there is a psychological connection to dairy food and many people are emotionally attached. Personally, I know when I miss my mom I crave dairy products. Soft, creamy dairy is the ultimate comfort food. Ask anyone who has recently lost a love relationship, and between spoonfuls of ice-cream, their sad story of loss and loneliness will emerge.

Emotionally, dairy food takes me back to my mother where she cradles and nurtures me. The problem with this kind of thinking is that the cow is NOT my mother. Unless, of course, my father had a barnyard fetish!

It's time to wean the adult body (and mind) off the nipple, stand on our own two feet, and face problems as they come. I suggest instead of diving into a pint of ice-cream for comfort and consolation, head straight back to the source and opt for a nourishing, mom-hug instead of a big bowl of baby cow food. If mom is not available, there may be other people like dad, brother, sister, spouse, or a good friend. A fantastic bonus when using hugs instead of food is that the hug is satisfying on a deeper level of consciousness, and has no calories. Hugging and human touch are powerful healing tools.

If you feel up to the task of letting go of dairy, put down this book (momentarily, of course), open the refrigerator, pour the skim milk down the drain and toss out the low-fat cottage cheese, then find someone you love and wrap your arms around them and give, and receive, a delicious hug. Hugs are instant gratification; as you hug, you get hugged right back. To better reclaim your health it's time to make intimate human connections and put that darn cow out to pasture!

One of the greatest fears of letting go of dairy stems from the idea that the only way to obtain adequate calcium is from milk products. The influence of the dairy industry (and the FDA, USDA) has led us to believe that the best place to get this mineral is from a cow.

Humans like any other living creature, need calcium to build strong bones and teeth, and to keep the blood and body alkaline balanced. Cows and other mammals need calcium too, so where do they derive calcium to build their bones? To find the answer I went to nature and observed the animals.

I want you to visualize a horse with its massive body of muscles, strong bones and great teeth. The horse does *not* run over to the barn in the middle of the night, wrestle the cow to the ground, flip it over and drink it's milk for calcium! After the young colt has been properly weaned from the nipple, it moves on to eat the food that it is designed to…grass, flowers, and other foods.

According to an article in Better Nutrition Magazine: "Broccoli, green beans, cauliflower and kale, although not cup-for-cup as high in calcium as milk, metabolize differently in the system, providing *more* calcium than milk."[7]

There is an abundance of high quality, bone-building calcium in all leafy green vegetables, sea vegetables, beans, grains, nuts, and seeds. Dairy food is *not* the *most* absorbable source of calcium for humans.

My friend Dina loves it when I talk about dairy and how it can create a glue-like substance (phlegm) in the body. The thought originates from kindergarten class when I learned how to make a piñata. It was easy… I took refined white flour (or any flour) and mixed it with milk to create a sticky, gluey substance that was used to paste shredded newspaper onto shaped cardboard. There are many different combinations of piñata glue that can be created inside the body at every meal: bagel with cream cheese, pizza, any sandwich with cheese on it, cookies and milk, penne a la vodka, donuts and café latte, and much more. The list is long and sticky! A great reminder of how dairy affects the body can be found on a bottle of Elmer's Glue… there's a little cow's head on the label.

---

[7] Mineral Medicine, by Rita Robinson, Better Nutrition Magazine, July 1999, page 36

Don't get me wrong, a little bit of gluey, gooey food is fun and not detrimental to overall health, but consuming it on a daily basis, three times a day can cause a mucous mess inside the body. For healing purposes, it's best to stay away from dairy products until the body becomes lean and clean, and then, a little bit of good quality, organic hormone-free dairy can be consumed, if desired.

When it comes to dairy products I practice moderation because I have lived through its effect on my body (overweight, allergies, excess mucus, pimples, etc.). Occasionally, I'll have yogurt, kefir, butter, ghee or naturally aged raw cheese, but I certainly don't eat it three times per day! If I resumed consuming dairy food the way I used to, I could wind up right back where I started – chubby like a baby, and more likely plagued with illness.

Beyond infancy, I wanted to discover what else I was physically designed to eat. Michio Kushi, a pioneer in Macrobiotic eating says, "The structure of the human teeth offers another biological clue to humanity's natural way of eating. The thirty-two teeth include 20 molars and pre-molars for grinding grains, legumes, and seeds; 8 incisors for cutting vegetables; and 4 canines for tearing animal and seafood. Expressed as a ratio of teeth designed for grain use, for vegetable use, and for animal use, the proportion comes to 5:2:1; and of all vegetable quality to animal quality, 7:1."[8]

I have four canines, twenty molars (actually sixteen molars and four root canals due to excess sugar consumption!) and eight incisors, indicating I am physically designed as an *omnivore*. Going against the

---

[8] The Book of Macrobiotics, Michio Kushi, Japan Publications, 1986, p.78.

body's physical structure can create illness in humans, as well as animals too.

A dear friend, a strict vegetarian, was so immersed in the principles behind adopting a plant-based diet, that she forced her view of life onto her dogs. Not taking into account their physical design, she fed them only vegetable foods. After a time, one of the dogs developed a serious nervous disorder, and the other suffered persistent skin rashes. Dogs are physically designed as omnivores with an emphasis on eating mostly animal foods (they have many canines!). Giving a dog food that goes against its design eventually results in physical problems.

Another great example is the cow: a natural herbivore. Factory farmers have been feeding cows ground up meat to fatten them, and it's also a good way to get rid of the "downed" cows (sick animals that die before they get to the slaughterhouse). Besides being unethical, this goes against the "laws of nature" and consequently, cows have developed illnesses like mad cow disease. Since the occurrence of mad cow disease it is currently illegal to feed a cow back to a cow, but factory farmers can still legally feed them other animal carcasses like chicken, fish, sheep, and road kill. This is terribly wrong, inhumane, and should be illegal, but it's not.

I too, experienced the effect of not eating according to my physical structure. During my initial change in diet I had eliminated almost all animal foods except a small amount of fish weekly. Eating mostly vegetable foods, rich in fiber, helped my body cleanse: I lost weight, the goiter (thyroid) shrank and eventually disappeared, and my skin glowed.

After a time, I then chose complete veganism (no animal food at all). I read many vegetarian texts on health and spirit that espoused abstaining from animal food to obtain a cleaner body and a closer union with God. I decided to try it.

Initially, I lost more weight and felt lighter in both body and mind – I felt great! "It was working," or so I thought. Within one year of adopting a completely vegan diet an odd thing began to happen; I felt an overall weakness, tingling, and sometimes sharp burning sensation in my muscles. It wasn't the usual feeling that resulted from exertion during exercise, but felt as if the muscle was eating itself away. I also lost strength and vitality, and became flaccid. My hair started graying prematurely, I battled Candida yeast chronically, and my immune system crashed; frequent cold sores popped up again. Egads!

Intuitively, I knew something was wrong and searched within my diet to figure out the root cause. Various vegetarian websites and resource groups recommended supplementing with vitamin B12, calcium and other vitamins and minerals. I don't believe in taking supplements (except for very short-term use when it's absolutely needed). Isolated vitamins are not whole foods, and can initially alleviate a symptom, but will eventually cause other problems to develop because they lack the full range of elements (fiber, water, fat, other vitamins & minerals) to be properly absorbed and digested. Also, no living creature on this planet needs vitamin supplementation for **great** health, and if I were eating a completely balanced diet, then I wouldn't need supplementation either. I believe nature provides me with *everything* I need to sustain my existence, in my daily food. Period.

As a vegan I ate vegetable foods that contained trace amounts of vitamin B12, and tons of calcium and other vitamins and minerals, but possibly my body wasn't fully absorbing them without the saturated fat and other necessary factors. I read that vitamin B12 is *best* absorbed through the process of eating animal foods, but I had abstained from eating it believing it was the ideal way and morally right. I was certainly in a quandary; my physical body felt deficient and contrary to what I had read in the vegetarian diet textbooks I knew I had to resume eating some good quality animal foods again. I was wrought with conflict and guilt.

I had to resolve this dilemma, so I went to a "healthy fast food" restaurant that served organic, pasture-raised meats. I hadn't eaten red meat in many years and I was nervous as heck! Literally, I stood inside the restaurant for about twenty minutes and stared up at the menu on the wall. The young guy standing behind the counter asked me two or three times if I needed some help, and I couldn't answer. The mere thought of eating an animal paralyzed me. I walked back outside the restaurant and paced up and down the block a few times contemplating my actions, and then returned to the restaurant and stood in line again.

The same guy looked at me and said, "Can I take your order?"

I shook my head and continued staring up at the menu.

"Uhmm… are you okay?"

I shook my head again. I was facing a crucial moment in my life. I abstained from eating animal flesh because I believed this would give me the best possible health, and bring me closer to "God," and I was about to commit the biggest sin! I turned around and walked right back out the door again. I paced up and down the block a few times, but knew I had to trust my intuition and how I felt *inside* my body, and not something I read *inside* a book.

I walked back into the restaurant. The same guy stared at me, with his eyebrows raised, but didn't ask to take my order this time.

I spoke first. "Let me ask you this… do you like the turkey or beef burger better?"

He laughed, "Well, I'm a beef man, myself. Turkey doesn't really do it for me. It's not juicy enough."

I ordered the beef burger and figured if I was going to sin, I might as well make it a juicy one. I sat down at a table and played with the ketchup while waiting for my order, and the devil, to arrive.

The server brought my meal and I unwrapped the burger to inspect it. It was slick with animal fat, and juicy too, just as described. I inhaled deeply. It smelled like a barbecue on a hot summer day. I salivated. Then, I cut off a little piece, and held it on the edge of my fork, turning it around and around as if it were on a spigot, and inspected it even more closely. Then… I put it into my mouth. I thought a lightning bolt would surely come through the front door and knock me off my chair! But it didn't. I chewed the meat and noticed it had a mildly sweet flavor. As I chewed I consciously gave blessings of gratitude to the animal for its life, and also thanked the mesclun greens and coleslaw too.

I did not feel any difference immediately after eating the meat, but a funny thing happened about twenty minutes later while walking down the block. A surge of energy traveled down the front of both my legs and extended all the way down to the tips of my toes. It was exhilarating! And, one hour after the meal I had a strong burst of energy throughout my entire body. That night I slept solidly, and the following morning awoke feeling exceptionally vibrant. The best part was I still felt connected to my spirituality, and my morning meditation was deeper. My experience with the hamburger contradicted many of the things I had read.

It's been quite a few years since that incident and I've continued eating animal foods because there is an energy in it that I can't deny – whether it's from the B12 or not, the science behind it I don't really know. What I do know is that my body feels healthier and stronger with animal food. Today, I wisely use the energy from both the animal and vegetable kingdoms, in the right proportions for me, to create vibrant health.

A quick look at many people living in large meat eating cultures reveals that animal foods might contribute to a strong, thick body and bones. People living in northern or colder climates (Russia, Alaska, Poland, etc.) have relied on heavy animal food that builds a dense body and protects against the harsh elements.

Plant based food, fruit, and most fish, generally cools and cleanses the body. This can be observed in warmer tropical climates where people usually have thinner bodies and bone structure, and eat more vegetables and fruits.

The majority of the world's population lives in a temperate climate with four to five seasons and variations of hot and cold weather. To obtain the best health in a temperate climate, a balanced diet would include mostly plant-based foods with smaller amounts of animal food. And, it makes sense to have more animal food in fall and winter, and more vegetables and fruits during spring and summer.

In general, animal food "builds" the body and vegetable food "cleanses" the body. I've observed this building process specifically with pregnant women.

I had a friend who was vegan for over ten years and within thirty days of becoming pregnant she had intense cravings for meat and started eating hamburgers. Similar meat cravings appeared when my best friend,

Jeannie, became pregnant (she was vegan for 3 years). And, yet another macrobiotic friend informed me she had insatiable cravings for turkey during her pregnancy.

Later, as I began to counsel people about health, I witnessed those same strong animal food cravings with other pregnant vegetarian, vegan and macrobiotic clients. There's no doubt in my mind that animal food builds the body, and pregnant women are doing just that: building little bodies.

If I'm *not* pregnant or *not* living in a harsh, cold environment, and I ingest *excessive* amounts of animal protein I could be building an overweight condition or growing other things inside my body like tumors, cysts, hardened masses, or congested arteries. To obtain great health we need to find the proper balance of both animal and vegetable foods. And, for a temperate climate (four to five seasons) I highly suggest eating a predominantly plant-based diet with smaller amounts of animal food, similar to a traditional Asian diet.

Our current approach to eating is off balance, and as a result, our bodies are too. But, by taking the time to look into nature and research the facts, we can make the choices that make the most sense.

I transitioned my diet to one in accordance with my physical design and climate, and my body and mind are stronger than ever, as a bonus, I physically look better now than during my twenties! Once you make the switch, you'll start to feel and look better too.

Another vital aspect to healing my body was changing the *quality* of my food. Food is an energy source and I needed the best quality energy to heal. The next chapter reviews the energy from food and where you can derive the greatest sources.

CHAPTER VI
E = QUALITY OF FOOD

Albert Einstein said that everything in the universe is energy…
including us. Energy emanates from every cell in the entire body, even
while sleeping, and it doesn't cease until the last breath. While we're
alive, we need to fuel ourselves with energy because that is what we are.

Before I changed my eating habits, I had no idea there was any
"energy" inside my body, at least not until I drank my first cup of coffee in
the morning! I remember dragging myself out of bed completely
exhausted, even though I had a full night's sleep, and needing extreme
foods like caffeine and sugar to kick-start my engine. And then,
throughout the day, I needed periodic caffeine and sugar hits to keep me
motoring along.

Today, I don't drink coffee or other highly caffeinated drinks
because I don't need to. When I changed the quality of fuel in my system,
my energy levels improved, and the overall quality of my life improved
too.

ABC Primetime News covered a story about a Japanese village
where the residents enjoyed long, healthy lives. They had no need to see
the town doctor and continued physically working at jobs well into their
late eighties and nineties. The older population ate locally grown starches
and vegetables as their main meal, with fish and meat as supplemental

foods. The younger generation, however, adopted the Western way of indulging in highly processed and refined foods, and excess meat and dairy, and they have suffered dire consequences.

"Komori (the town doctor) points to statistics that since Western-style processed food infiltrated the village a few years ago, heart disease has doubled. With youngsters being seduced by these products, what the Japanese call an upside-down death pyramid has emerged, in which adults die before their elderly parents."[9]

The notorious American "death pyramid" is proving food has the ability to either keep the body functioning at full capacity for a long and healthy life, or congest the body and cease its energy flow.

The food I eat breaks down through the process of digestion and becomes my blood, cells, flesh, organs and most importantly, my mind. What I eat or drink makes me grow physically and emotionally. Hence the age-old sayings: "food for thought," and "you are what you eat."

Knowing that food creates my physical body, I can use highly energized food as a tool to change on a cellular level, from the inside out. If there's any doubt about that, chew on this… what makes the human body grow? An infant cannot become a fully-grown adult without the process of absorbing food. If the food I ate during childhood passed right through me, I would have remained an infant, or died of malnutrition. Food does not pass directly through my body - it goes through an intricate assimilating process, and actually becomes part of my body (discarding the waste, of course).

Food energy is transferred into the person eating or drinking it. Alcohol is a great example of an *extremely* refined food that lacks

---

[9]The Village of Long Life, ABC News.com, November 2, 2002

substantial nutrients and energy. Alcohol becomes the body on a cellular level, and if taken in excess can cause loss of motor movements and coordination, slurred speech, lack of concentration, emotional problems and much more.

I discovered that the healthier I became, the more I could feel the weakening effect of alcohol. This is another one of the foods I use in moderation because it tends to give me a headache (too much sugar) and can make me feel groggy the next day. Alcohol is a nutritionally deficient food that doesn't supply sustainable energy.

Food takes the same passageway into my body as alcohol, except it doesn't have as obvious or as immediate an effect. Eventually, the accumulation of all foods and their effects on the body, either good or bad, show up.

If your goal is to reclaim your health, have more energy and look and feel your absolute best, one way to get there is by eating whole, nutrient rich, organic and locally grown foods. "Whole food" hasn't been highly refined or processed; it's in its most natural, unadulterated state, straight from the earth and packed with vitamins, minerals, and energy. A complete list of specific whole foods and how to cook them can be found in **The Whole Truth Eating and Recipe Guide**.

When buying whole food (or any food) it's best to make it organic. Studies have proven that organically grown foods have higher levels of vitamins, minerals and antioxidants than conventionally grown. In the May 1999 issue of *Natural Health Magazine* (page 31) it states: "Men who eat organic foods produce forty-three percent more sperm than those who do not, according to a recent report published in the *Lancet*, a British medical journal." Reproductive capacity is considered the essence of life, and if organic food increases that energy, it's a good idea to incorporate it into your diet!

On the other hand, conventionally produced farmed foods are liberally sprayed with toxic chemicals: pesticides, herbicides, fungicides, insecticides and other poisons that cause a negative energetic effect in the food source, and inevitably, in your body too.

A great example: When I was growing up, I remember finding clusters of ants in the kitchen during the hot, summer months. The quick solution was to spray a bug killer (insecticide), like Raid to kill them. Below are some interesting facts, word for word, from the label on Raid Max Ant and Roach Killer.

The Raid Max tag line is, "Kills Fast, Kills Long." It also cautions:

- Spray away from self and other persons.
- **DO NOT** use in food processing plants, restaurants, or other areas where food is commercially prepared or processed.
- **DO NOT** use in serving areas while food is exposed. Remove birds and tightly cover fish bowls and aquariums.
- **DO NOT** allow pets in treated area.
- Hazards to humans and domestic animals.
- Harmful if absorbed through the skin. If on skin - wash with plenty of soap and warm water. Get medical attention if irritation persists.
- If swallowed: **CALL A PHYSICIAN OR POISON CONTROL CENTER IMMEDIATELY.**

I don't recall reading those warnings before spraying the insecticide, and I certainly didn't cover the fish bowl or put the pets outside! I just took aim and fired. Within seconds the ants flopped over, squirmed around, and died. Raid is powerful stuff and does exactly what it says, "Kills Fast!"

After spraying the insecticide I clearly remember something else happened. My eyes became red, itchy and teary, my nose ran, and my throat closed up. My body attempted to discharge the chemicals I had unwittingly (or more appropriately, dimwittingly) ingested. For my own protection, I left the room as quickly as possible, and went outside for fresh air so I could breathe again.

Factory farmed produce is sprayed with far more toxic chemicals than Raid Ant Killer. Plants are alive, but they cannot uproot themselves and go elsewhere to get fresh air as I did.

Besides losing nutritional value from this process, the produce becomes contaminated with deadly chemicals that cannot be washed off because they're actually *inside* the food itself. Soil and water are doused with pesticides, and the produce uses that soil and water to grow. "You are what you eat" does not apply solely to humans!

The amount of pesticide residue on produce pales in comparison to the quantity in meat and dairy products. Pesticides are highly stable substances that do not break down in the environment or in the body, and accumulate in fat cells as we ascend the food chain. What makes this information especially frightening is at the very top of the food chain, accumulating the highest amounts of chemical contaminant is MAN. "Man" includes men, women and children too.

Some health risks associated with pesticide buildup include cancer, genetic mutations, birth defects, brain damage, liver damage, and other organ damage.[9] The chemicals in our food supply are definitely *not* health promoting. Why the government allows these deadly poisons to be used on our food is a mystery, and I can only assume that it's benefiting someone financially... at the very *top* of the food chain.

Make no mistake about it, pesticides, herbicides, fungicides and insecticides are harsh chemicals designed to **kill** bugs. One major difference between human beings and bugs is we are BIGGER. It may take longer, but eventually, those same deadly chemicals used to kill the little bugs, will kill us too.

I believe people dousing the food supply with poisonous substances possibly commit homicide with every application, and by eating these fatal foods we commit suicide with every bite! Eating chemicals creates toxic waste inside the body, and is *not* the best way to reclaim your health.

Another serious food issue is genetically modified (GM and GMO) food otherwise known as "Frankenfoods." GM foods are designed in laboratories and have not evolved in the natural environment. These foods have *never* been a part of the human diet and are proving to negatively effect the body.

GM nightmares include Bovine Growth Hormone (rBGH) administered to cows to increase milk production, but it also produces tumors, udder infections, mastitis, reproductive disorders and shortens the life span of the animal.[10] If I eat food from a diseased, chemically

---

[9] Diet For a New America, By John Robbins
[10] Imagine a World Without Monarch Butterflies, by Alex Jack.

contaminated, and poorly treated animal, it will have a detrimental effect on my health.

The FDA ruled that GM foods do *not* need to be labeled. This has resulted in more than 75% of processed foods in grocery stores already containing these dangerous foods and the consumer doesn't know it. Avoiding GM foods can be tricky, but a good rule of thumb is to eat *organic* and avoid most or all processed foods that contain soy, corn, canola, cottonseed and dairy because these are the most widely contaminated. Some common everyday foods that contain GM ingredients include popcorn, tortillas, corn syrup, corn fructose, high fructose corn syrup, dextrose, corn oil, corn chips, cookies, candies and gums, breads and baked goods, alcohol, enriched flours and pastas, salad dressings, soy foods, tofu, soymilk, soy isolates, soy proteins, soy hotdogs, soy burgers, soy cheese, ice cream, frozen yogurt, milk, butter, sour cream, buttermilk, cottage cheese, yogurt, chocolate, breakfast cereals, protein powders, infant formulas, cosmetics, potatoes, tomatoes, squash, radicchio, french fries, mashed potatoes, potato chips, tomato sauce and pizza.

The list is long, and the health concerns are even longer! As illness and disease statistics continue mounting, American consumers have become unwitting guinea pigs in these GM experiments on the food supply.

Almost all meat, dairy, poultry and fish are raised on feed that is genetically modified unless it's labeled "organically fed," or it's from a local farmer you can trust. **Organic** labeling excludes the use of GM ingredients. It's time for consumers to say NO to GM foods and buy organic!

New clients often tell me they don't want to buy organic food because it costs more. To make my point I offer this scenario:

There are two boats on the shore and I need to buy one of them to take an eighty-five year (or longer) journey on the river of life. The first boat costs $150 and has been doused with chemicals that will surely rot the wood and cause it to sink before the journey is complete. The second boat costs $350, but the wood is clean, strong and durable, ensuring a safer journey. Which one would you buy? I highly suggest you spend the extra money and buy the better boat (organic foods), and continue your voyage as safely as possible. It's a wise investment in your health, and you're worth it.

Eating seasonally and locally are other great ways to create internal balance and obtain vital energy from food. Each season produces food that grows at a specific time of year in a specific area, making it the perfect food to eat then.

Locally grown, seasonal foods taste better and fresher than food shipped from thousands of miles away. The smartest chefs in the best restaurants understand this simple philosophy. They usually buy their produce from local suppliers and change their menus accordingly with each season.

We live in a country where everything is available at any time, but this does not mean we should eat those foods all year round. Before changing my diet I had no idea what grew in my area because I was completely removed from the process of planting and harvesting. I only knew that food was available all year inside the supermarket regardless of the season. I could buy watermelon mid-winter, and if it was there, it must be good for me. I was wrong!

Imagine this scenario: I used to come home from work on an icy, cold winter day, remove my scarf, gloves, hat, winter jacket, and thick layers of warm clothing, and head into the kitchen for dinner. After rubbing my palms together to generate warmth and stave off frostbite, I ate a dinner that consisted of cool, refreshing watermelon, strawberries and other fruit, and a salad of iceberg lettuce, cucumbers, tomatoes and low-fat dressing, and then maybe some tuna salad with low-fat mayo on fat-free white bread.

Looking back at that meal, I understand why my body was completely out of balance and in a state of dis-ease. Watermelon, strawberries, iceberg lettuce, cucumbers, and tomatoes, do *not* grow in the winter in New York. Those foods are grown in Mexico, Florida, California or other warm environments, and are shipped to New York during winter. Cooling summer fruits and salads are *not* the best foods for me to eat when it's freezing outside, and consequently I was always cold, frequently sick and never had any energy. All of my energy reserves went toward trying to heat my body.

Better winter fruit choices for me in my particular environment would have been pears and apples. And, sautéed hearty winter, greens like kale, cabbage, and collards would have been better for me than an iceberg lettuce salad. Even the name "ice-berg" is cold!

Here's another example to give you a clear picture. The Eskimo lives in an extremely frigid environment where not much vegetation grows, but is able to thrive eating animal foods like caribou, snow rabbit, whale blubber, seals, fatty fish, birds and eggs. These foods produce strong, warming energy, and help to insulate his body against the cold. If the Eskimo were to retire and move to Florida (where many retirees dwell) and continue eating *large* quantities of warming animal foods his health would quickly deteriorate and his physical condition would become overheated and overweight.

An environmentally balanced diet for a warmer climate like Florida includes large quantities of fresh fruit and vegetables, fish and smaller amounts of other animal foods. If the Native Floridian were to move to Alaska and continue to eat a diet that consisted of raw salads, grapefruits and oranges, before long he would surely freeze to death!

Incorporating foods that are available in each season enabled my body to become harmonious with the environment, helping me to better physically adapt to my surroundings. After I became more balanced by eating seasonally, I found I could no longer tolerate air-conditioning. I did not want to ride the subway or city buses in the summer because they were like rolling meat lockers and I would freeze my buns off! It was a blessing actually, because I started walking everywhere, incorporating more exercise.

Temperate climate dwellers (people living with four to five seasons) are the majority of the world's population, and can eat a wide variety of foods, making slight adjustments to the diet as the weather changes: adding more warming animal food in the winter and more cooling plant-based foods in the summer. A list of temperate climate foods and how to cook them is covered in *The Whole Truth Eating and Recipe Guide.*

For a better understanding of what grows in your area of the world, visit your local farmers market (**www.ams.usda.gov/farmersmarkets**) during each specific season or join a **Community Supported Agriculture. (www.localharvest.org)**. A CSA consists of people that buy directly

70

from the farmer – it helps support local farmers, and in the process supports health too!

What the farmer near you is harvesting is what you should be eating at that time of year. And remember… just because something is available in the supermarket all year round does not make it the best food for your health.

It can still be healthy to have summer foods in the winter, and winter foods in the summer, but remember to make the *majority* of your food what is growing in the environment around you; what the earth naturally provides. This way of eating creates balance between the external environment and your internal environment, and helps to strengthen your system as a whole.

Choose food that make sense; eat organic, wholesome, local and seasonal to help you reclaim your health, increase your energy, and reach your ideal weight. Freedom from illness can be a reality when you learn how to supply your body with the best quality foods possible. Trust me, your health is worth it.

After I changed my quality of food, I realized it's just as important, if not more so, to adjust quality of life and nourish other parts of my sensory self as well. There is more to life than just food!

CHAPTER VII
<u>SATISFYING THE SENSES</u>

I reclaimed my health by altering my diet to one that was more wholesome, nutrient rich, organic and seasonal, but I soon discovered that FOOD alone was *not* the answer to everything. Other parts of my body and mind, besides my stomach and digestive organs, needed proper nourishment too: what I ingest through my senses can have a positive or negative effect on health.

A short while after my one-year sabbatical from media (television, newspapers, movies, etc), I watched a horror movie with a friend. I quickly realized I couldn't view the violent images of people being killed. The images caused a sharp pain in my heart, and made me feel physically sick even though the movie was fictional.

The scenes of human beings maiming, dismembering, and killing other humans were unsettling (to say the least) so I closed my eyes during the "bad" parts. I also found the slashing, ripping and screaming sounds was too much for me, but unfortunately couldn't cover both eyes and ears simultaneously.

Halfway through the film, I opened my eyes before a gory scene was finished and saw a man bleeding from both of his eyes, with blood dripping down his cheeks. I felt pain in my chest and a surge of nausea at that very instant, but after leaving the movie didn't think about it again. The movie was over and the scene was finished… or so I thought.

When I lay down in bed that night, I couldn't stop that one particular image from flashing in my mind's eye. The bloody scene persisted for two entire weeks. Whenever I closed my eyes, there it was again and again, and each time I saw it, it physically weakened me.

Abstaining from violent images increased my sensitivity; I could no longer stomach them. What made this discovery highly unusual was I grew up watching, and loving, horror films – they were my favorite genre and I watched them almost every night!

When I first met Michio Kushi for my Macrobiotic health evaluation, he advised me to "*not*" watch the evening news if I wanted to heal my thyroid. I didn't understand the concept back then, but I understand it today. The news is thirty minutes long and most of it reports everything *wrong* happening in the world. If I absorb those images and thoughts into my mind/body and believe the entire world is in a terrible state and everyone is killing everyone **all** the time, then I could lose my hope for life, and with that my ability and desire to heal.

If you are healing an illness I highly suggest you become selective about what you absorb through your eyes, ears, nose, mouth, and skin. All of your senses are entryways into your body and mind, and can positively or negatively affect your health.

Examine your personal environment and figure out what you're observing on a daily basis. Are you sitting in an enclosed, gray colored office with no windows, staring at a computer screen? Are there plants or pictures of people you love on your desk? Are you watching people destroy each other in violent movies, or on the nightly news before going to bed? What are the final images you see before laying down to rest and rejuvenate?

We may be living in big cities surrounded by concrete and steel, but we are still a part of nature and need to be surrounded by natural beauty and energy to help balance out the many unnatural things in our environment.

Plants in particular, besides adding color to the world, give us oxygen and in return we give them carbon. It's a symbiotic relationship; they nourish us and we nourish them! Fill up your house and office with green plants and take a daily walk in the park, or a weekly hike in the mountains. Your eyes, lungs, and the rest of your body will love you for it. Take a moment, right now, and observe your surroundings. Where can you place a plant?

What you hear affects your health. Are you listening to soothing sounds and music you love, or is your audio space filled with loud, offensive noise? Can you shut off the television and the radio, and listen to the sound of your own voice for a few moments? What do you sound like? Open your mouth and say this out loud, "ahhhhhhhhhhh." That's your voice.

It's time to relax and breathe for a moment or two. Try this simple task a couple of times per week (or daily if possible): turn off *everything,* sit in a comfortable chair, in silence for a few minutes and just breathe. Close your eyes and follow your breath as you inhale and exhale. Feel the air enter into your nose, travel down the back of your throat and bring it into your belly. Be conscious of carrying your breath all the way down into the center of your body, expand your abdomen and breathe like a baby.

74

I used to think it was normal to breathe up into my chest, but it's not. And, it took much practice to retrain myself how to properly breathe! I know it sounds like a simple concept, but it can have an incredible effect on your physical and emotional health. Meditation and deep breathing can quiet racing thoughts, helping to make your inner voice and intuition clear.

With time, the internal stillness and quietude you create can enable you to listen to your body and decipher its ailments. Is your body aching, creaking, cracking? Is it tired, overworked, exhausted or overweight? Stop what you are doing, sit still, breathe, and listen. What is your body telling you? The closer you get to the center of yourself the healthier you can become.

There are many great books on meditation that can teach you to quiet your mind. You don't need to join a monastery or run off to a secluded beach somewhere to find the place and the peace to heal. Peace is not anywhere outside of you, it's inside you - always. If you can learn to create a peaceful healing space within yourself you will be better able to understand the root cause of many health problems.

People, places and things in your external environment affect health too. It takes practice to successfully navigate negative situations and not let them have detrimental effects on your well-being. Until you locate your "center" and learn how to stay in it, you may have to distance yourself from people, places and things that are harmful; bad relationships can be as toxic as pesticide-coated food!

The people in our life (no matter how big or small) can teach us valuable lessons if we remain open to learning. I discovered how important it is to stop and smell the flowers from my six-year nephew, Danny. We were walking down a busy city street and passed a local market with bunches of brightly colored, pink, purple, red, yellow and orange flowers on display. Danny told me to stop and smell the flowers, so I bent down and *pretended* to smell them and then nonchalantly continued walking.

Danny stamped his feet and yelled, "NO, Aunt Fanny, you have to really stop and *smell* the flowers!"

I laughed at his insistence, but then stopped to really smell those flowers. They were sweet and fragrant, and each had a distinctive aroma that stirred another sensation inside my body and mind. That simple yet powerful, olfactory experience was brought to my attention by a young boy who was not rushing to get somewhere else, but was present to that very moment in his life. It only took a couple of seconds to really smell those flowers, but it heightened my awareness and invigorated me.

For healing (and living) purposes, it's essential to feel, feel, and feel some more! Feel the wind in your hair and the rain on your skin. Leave the office or the house and get out to enjoy the sunshine. Turn your face up toward the sky and let the sun kiss you – it's a healthy dose of Vitamin D and can help lift depression too.

Fully feel everything you can with all of your external (five senses) and internal (emotional) self. What does it feel like to hold someone you love? Is it warm and comforting? What does it feel like to be held by someone who loves you? Do you feel safe, secure, nourished? Can you feel their energy on your skin, or under your skin? How about in your heart? Try it – put down this book for a moment and hold someone in your arms. How did it feel, both physically and emotionally?

Observe a puppy bouncing down the street, bend down to touch its soft fur. How does it feel on the edges of your fingertips? If you're

76

feeling adventurous let that puppy lick your nose and your face. Have you ever noticed little kids giggling when puppies lick them? Try it yourself and see if it makes you giggle too.

Taste everything – don't just gobble food, because you'll lose the experience of it. Slow down and chew, learn how to be present with your food. Take a strawberry and hold it in your hand. Look at it. Touch it. Run your finger along the tiny beige seeds on the outside of its shiny, plump, red skin. Put the strawberry to your nose and inhale deeply. What does it smell like? Place the strawberry between your teeth and take a small nibble but don't swallow. Roll it around inside your mouth and feel the texture – is it firm on the outside and tender on the inside? Is it sweet and satisfying? Let that small piece of strawberry touch every part of your tongue and taste it before you gulp it down. If you could do this experiment with all of your food, it could satisfy your senses on a deeper level and you'll gain much *more* by eating much *less*. If you have access to a piece of fruit or some other food try this experiment right now and observe how you feel afterward. You may be surprised at what you discover.

Learning how to get in tune with your sense of sight, taste, touch, smell and hearing will enable you to get more closely connected to your inner self and you'll be better equipped to figure out what's occurring inside you. Not only that, but fine tuning your senses will heighten all of your daily experiences. Try it… you'll like it! I promise.

To naturally reclaim health it's imperative to experience our physical senses and decipher how to nourish them properly, but we also need to feed our emotional self. The emotional part of us may be starving, but we may unconsciously reach out for food as a substitute. Before you gobble down the next pint of ice-cream, or whatever food comforts you, ask yourself, "What do I really want right now? Am I bored, lonely, angry, sad, depressed, annoyed? Check in and distinguish if you are *physically* hungry or *emotionally* hungry. If it's the latter, figure out what else needs to be nourished in your life and feed it.

For example, what do you love to do more than anything in the world? What makes your heart soar; when you're doing it time flies? If you don't know what you love to do, take a class and try something new: Sing, dance, knit, play ball, cook a meal, do pottery, poetry, run, exercise, watch movies, act on stage, dine with friends, take a walk... whatever it is that you love, do it with all of your heart. Otherwise, what are you doing here?

Creating a health promoting lifestyle requires practice that's ongoing, but you can do it. Henry Ford (founder of Ford Motor company) had an eighth grade education and he said, "Whether you think you can or you think you can't, you're right." So what do you think? Do you think you can? I think you can. If I could do it, then you can do it too. As long as you are alive and breathing you can do anything!

Your daily thoughts about yourself are powerful. Just as "you are what you eat," creates your physical body, "you are what you think," creates your emotional body. If you think you are a bad person, you will be a bad person, and if you think you are not good enough, you won't be. Your thoughts have created who you are today, and they can create who you will be tomorrow. At this moment, what do you think about yourself? Take a deep breath and relax – you're alive, you're learning something new, you're beautiful.

When I realized I wanted to teach people how to reclaim their health, I knew I had to quit my corporate day job and create a whole new profession, but I was scared as heck! I had never taught before and doubted I could do it. My negative thoughts kept me stuck, unable to move forward. The task to teach kept gnawing at me continually. I knew people needed this information to make the world a better place, and my remaining small and insecure wasn't serving anyone.

It took six months of positive thinking, and retraining my thoughts, before I had the courage to take on teaching, motivating and inspiring. The transition didn't happen overnight. It was a process of gaining confidence and crowding out old negative beliefs that were no longer valid.

Today, I know I can do anything as long as I believe in myself. Positive thinking about your own situation, whatever it is, takes work and practice, but the end results are worth it for you and the world around you.

While healing, it's also a good idea to release any resentment you may have toward others. Someone once told me that holding on to resentment and anger is like drinking poison and expecting the other person to die. Egads! That's a compelling thought. One of the most healing activities you can do for your mind, body and soul, is to forgive.

Release negative thoughts from the past and let go of what happened yesterday; you can never change it. Dwelling on the past can keep you stuck and eventually lead to depression. In the past lives the phrases, "I should have, could have, and would have." You can't change what happened in the past, but you can learn from it and try not to make the same choices in the present.

My past unhealthy life and food choices weren't mistakes - they were valuable lessons that taught me *how to* create a dis-eased condition through lack of self-care, poor food choices and detrimental lifestyle habits. Today I know what NOT to eat or do in my daily life if I want to obtain true freedom from illness.

If you are an emotional eater (like many people, including me!) and reach out for cookies, donuts, ice cream and junk food, it will inevitably create an overweight or dis-eased condition. Emotional eating will persist until you get to the root cause of the problem. In the meantime you could make better food choices to overeat on until you understand how to properly deal with the triggers that set you off.

I've discovered that clients who hold on to negative thoughts about themselves or others, no matter how "well" they eat don't become healthy as quickly as people who change their way of thinking. Negative and positive thinking are learned behaviors. The more you practice the positive, the better you'll learn it and be able to use it to your advantage. There's healing power in positive thinking.

There are many ways to alter negative thoughts and it can begin with becoming conscious about what's happening in your life. Whatever you want to be, achieve or create begins with your consciousness and ability to make the best possible choices to promote your physical and emotional health on a daily basis.

If you're working at a job you hate, QUIT! That's right... I said it! If you wake up everyday and spend eight to ten hours (or longer) doing work you don't like, and your heart is not in it, that job can negatively affect your body and mind. Unless you find something to like about your work, you may be better off doing something else. At the end of the day nothing matters if you don't like what you do, and chances are, if you don't like what you do with the majority of your time, you won't like *you* either. Finding work you enjoy can be highly beneficial to your health.

Learn how to really live your life. Living doesn't mean watching television and living vicariously through the lives of movie actors and television shows; it means getting out of the house and getting into your own life. This is not a rehearsal - this is your life, and its time for you to become the superstar! You are a magnificent creation and it is your divine right to enjoy a fully engaged existence.

Believe in yourself. Ralph Waldo Emerson said, "If I have lost confidence in myself, I have the universe against me." On the other hand, if you have confidence and believe in yourself you will have the entire universe working with you to manifest your dreams. That's a pretty big support system!

Other lifestyle suggestions include reading a great book (like this one!), learning how to cook, giving or getting a massage as often as possible, surrounding yourself with people you love, laughing out loud, crying all the way down to the depth of your soul, exercising your body and mind, and experiencing nature as often as possible. And, while you're out and about in the world experiencing nature open your eyes, observe its beauty, and then open your heart and absorb it with your senses.

Everyday we have a new opportunity to fully live life. Don't wait until tomorrow, or next week, or until you have enough money, or until a sickness grows in your body.... change your life right now, today. Learn how to be present and experience all of your senses every moment while you're alive, or you may miss out on a lot of fantastic things - one of them being vibrant health.

Most importantly, learn how to truly love and accept yourself in the body you're living in right now. When you love yourself it's much easier to take care of yourself. You can start loving yourself by making the time to commit to the self-care and responsibility vital to reclaiming your health. By committing to better quality choices, ongoing, you can transform your life.

CHAPTER VIII
MAKE A COMMITMENT TO YOU!

My diseased condition could not have changed if I had not taken full responsibility for my health, and incorporated a plan of action to achieve my desired goals. I had subconsciously (or consciously) created my illness with unwholesome eating and lifestyle habits, and I cured it by changing those self-destructive ways.

I made the connection; I have *one* body for my *entire* life. If I had only one pair of pants for my entire life, I would have to take exceptional care of them! I needed to get serious and take exceptional care of my *one* body because I did *not* want to order any man-made replacement parts due to my lack of self-care and maintenance.

Taking responsibility for my health included not blaming advertisers or the makers of fast food and junk food for my unhealthy condition. Even though I was influenced by the media, fantastic advertising and many other forms of thought manipulation throughout my life, in the end, everything I ingested was my choice. No one forced me to eat nutrient-deficient substances.

According to Fox News on July 24th, 2002, a man sued McDonald's, Burger King, Wendy's and Kentucky Fried Chicken, claiming they were irresponsible and deceptive in their nutritional information. He was diabetic, with high blood pressure and high cholesterol, and consequently suffered two heart attacks. He blamed the fast food industry for his ailments, and said *they* needed to offer healthier options on their menus.

Fast food restaurants do *not* necessarily need to offer anything other than what they already offer. That man's ill health was a lack of responsibility to his own self-care and health maintenance. He created his physical condition with his choices, and gave away his health for the price of a Happy Meal!

Before I changed my disease-promoting behaviors, I too, refused to take full responsibility for my health, and my body and mind were a shambles. I remember waking every Monday morning swearing I would eat better or start another diet, but by noon my hand was already reaching for snack foods and stimulants!

I did what most dieters do; I reduced calories and restricted food intake, without changing the *quality* of my food. I set myself up for nutritional starvation. The food I was eating was crap, only now I was eating less of it!

My diet was nutrient poor and my lifestyle was disease promoting. I was eating junk food, drinking large quantities of alcohol at least two to three times per week, smoking cigarettes, and stimulating myself with caffeine and sugar all day long. I was *not* consistent with exercise, and had zero spiritual practice. These self-destructive behaviors added up to one thing... sickness in my body and mind. I was a physical and emotional wreck!

I know it may sound crazy but the greatest blessing came with my thyroid disease and the possibility of breast cancer. My body was unhealthy and it was my responsibility to bring it back to its rightful state:

vibrantly healthy. I knew I had to change my ways. No more excuses. No more "I'll start on Monday." I had to begin that day, not on New Year's Day, not next week, and not on my birthday. If I didn't commit to taking full responsibility for my health, I would inevitably become just another medical statistic, and would probably suffer a similar fate as my mother's.

Throughout my life, I was the biggest offender of broken commitments to myself, and other people, too. You couldn't depend on me for anything. I would make commitments to people and not show up, or be late with an excuse for one thing or another. I was not true to my word, and my broken commitments were a reflection of how I treated myself too. My way of living was not a good way to interact in the world.

Reclaiming my health began by making a commitment to myself. Without a healthier "me" at the helm of this boat (my body), my journey on the river of life would probably be cut short.

Committing to taking care of myself wasn't about living forever - it was about making the best choices as often as possible to achieve the best results, and having a better overall quality of life. When I committed to my health, my life transformed monumentally.

Clients often complain that they don't have enough time to take care of themselves because they have to care for a spouse, the kids, the job, or work late nights or weekends. Each time I hear an excuse, I can hear my old voice echoing in theirs. The truth is, by not *making the time* to care for their health right now, sickness and dis-ease will eventually take root and grow, and there won't be any time to care for anyone else, or to work the extra hours, or to make any more excuses!

Making a commitment is about *creating* the space where excuses aren't allowed to exist. There are no excuses, only choices. If you make better choices, consistently, better results are sure to follow. Taking on your health is no small potatoes (organic of course), but the more you do it the easier it will become.

Transitioning your diet and lifestyle may seem intimidating at first, but keep in mind that change can be a really good thing. Just as the caterpillar changes into a beautiful butterfly, you too can change.

At the time of my illness, I was working at a full time, high-stress job in New York City. It was a far cry from a "healing environment," but I consciously brought my health promoting ideals with me, wherever I went, to help me make the best choices anywhere, anytime. Reclaiming my health wasn't outside of me; it was inside me and in my daily choices.

Before starting my day at the office, I committed to self-care at home. In the morning I exercised with light stretching or yoga, and ate a healthy whole foods breakfast. While breakfast was cooking, I packed up dinner from the night before and took it with me for lunch. Eventually, I acquired an understanding of what to eat, how much, and why, and could successfully and sensibly order in restaurants. Even after I became "restaurant savvy" I still chose to bag my own lunch; it was the food I enjoyed, and made me feel great when I ate it and even better afterwards.

I committed to better quality food at every meal, and cooked as often as possible because I had a strong desire to change from the inside out. Food wasn't the only thing I changed on my agenda…. for the first time in my life I committed to a *daily* exercise program. Not two or three times a week at the gym, but moving my body in some way every single day, even if it was only a twenty minute walk. The combination of proper

86

diet plus regular exercise resulted in a strong healthy body, weight loss without dieting, and a firm rear end (as a nice added bonus!).

The subway ride from my apartment on the Upper East Side of Manhattan to the office in Midtown was fifty minutes on a good day. One day I put my sneakers on, packed my high heels in a bag, and walked my butt to work. It took fifty minutes to get there, exactly the same amount of time as if I had taken the subway. Although now, I no longer stood idle on the subway platform waiting to be packed into the train like a sardine, I was moving my body. By altering my routine from inaction to action, I arrived at the office highly energized and ready to start the day.

Walking to work cleared my mind, and increased my metabolism, and the next thing I knew, I wanted to walk everywhere all the time, including during my lunch hour. Making a commitment to using my feet has saved money on cabs, buses, subways, and gym memberships. I have invested that money elsewhere – in a great pair of walking shoes and organically grown foods. Rain or shine, if the mailman gets through then so could I! And, if I could do it, so can you.

Meditation became a daily part of my life too. I began with five minutes of sitting quietly a few times a week and slowly increased it. Sitting in silence gave me greater insight into myself, which is exactly what I needed to comprehend my true physical and emotional condition.

Connecting to myself through meditation enabled me to discover a healing intuition I didn't know I had – it's something we all have – every creature on the planet! We all know exactly what we need to thrive. Healing intuition is akin to a muscle and the more we use it the stronger it becomes.

These fundamental health-promoting tools helped me create a successful, dis-ease free life. In time, I glowed with radiant health and it motivated the people around me to take positive actions. I've discovered the old adage to be true... leading by example is the best way to initiate change in the world.

Today, I understand that my life is a continuous work in progress and each new ailment can bring with it greater insight and an opportunity to change and grow again and again. I'm not afraid to step up and make commitments to myself or to other people anymore, and I'm living at the greatest level of health and consciousness I have ever known. Making commitments and honoring them can bring about amazing life transformations.

I am acutely aware of what I say to people; if I say I'm going to do something, I do it. My words and actions are in alignment. Breaking my word can destroy my integrity and eventually erode my sense of self, bringing me right back where I started: physically and emotionally unhealthy. What I do to other people, I do to myself, and vice-versa. Becoming a fully functioning "healthy" human being is no longer a dream for me... it's my waking reality. It can be yours, too.

Okay… it's time to assess your present physical condition and ascertain where you might need to improve your life.

- Are you lacking energy and vitality?
- Do you have extreme swings in energy (high and low, not steady and balanced)
- Are you plagued with recurring colds and flus?
- Are you overweight?
- Is your skin tone and texture splotched, uneven, pasty or dull?
- Do you have high blood pressure or heart disease?
- Are you addicted to sugar and stimulants?
- Do you have diabetes or hypoglycemia?
- Do you have cancer or some other debilitating illness?

If you answered yes to *any* of the questions above, it's time to commit to you and your health! No matter what your current physical condition or situation is, I believe, as long as you are alive and breathing you can change it. You can create a health-promoting diet and lifestyle and realize your greatest living potential.

To reclaim and retain your health you will want to make some commitments to experience the ultimate transformation. Write down five or ten simple commitments to help you reach your health related goals, and read them every day; then do them to the best of your ability. Don't try to change everything at once and don't over commit yourself: it can be overwhelming.

If there is a huge mountain that needs to be moved, your thoughts of the tremendous task may paralyze you from taking action. But, if you pick up a small pile of rocks and move them one day at a time, eventually that entire mountain will be moved. Whatever that mountain is for you: sickness, disease, excess weight, lack of clarity and focus, it can be transformed with patience, persistence, love and commitment.

Some daily diet and lifestyle commitments can include:

- Transition your diet from junk foods and refined food to whole foods
- Buy organic whenever possible
- Pick out some tasty recipes from "*The Whole Truth –Eating and Recipe Guide*" or on the web at http://www.AndreaBeaman.com
- Cook and enjoy a fully balanced, nutritious meal two or three nights per week
- Take healthy dinner leftovers with you for lunch

Stop! Reread the list above and choose one thing (or more) you can do for yourself this week.

Okay, let's continue…

- Walk 25-30 minutes every day
- Exercise your mind with self-help books (like the one you're reading right now!)
- Honor yourself and make the best choices, consistently

- Shut off the television; get out of the sitcoms and get into your own life
- Practice deep breathing, meditation or prayer five minutes daily or a few times weekly

Take a deep breath and relax. The more you can incorporate any of the suggestions on these lists into your life, the easier it will get, and the healthier you will become. Take another deep breath and keep reading. You're doing great!

- Be conscious of what you say to people – if you say you're going to do something, do it
- Clean out closets and give away old clothes; you're going to need to make room for the new clothes to fit your improved body!
- Do something creative or take a class in painting, pottery, dancing, singing, writing, journaling, philosophy class, etc.
- Do the dishes before you go to bed – it will let you end the day with a completed project, and start the new day with a clean sink
- Create a healing space inside your body and mind

Choose one thing from the list above and see if you can apply it to your life today. And, finally...

- Love, love, love yourself as much as possible - when you love yourself, it's so much easier to take care of you

The last suggestion is *the* most important. Please incorporate self-love into your life as often as possible.

You can choose any (or all) of these health-promoting commitments or make your own and write them down on the Commitment Page at the end of this chapter. After you've made your commitments do not break them. But, if you do, *don't* beat yourself up over it. There is no self-healing with self-abuse. Becoming healthier takes time and practice. Be patient and loving with yourself while you're going through this process. Change doesn't happen overnight. Creating new positive habits takes time, but you will eventually crowd out old negative behaviors. Keep re-committing to yourself everyday and begin again, and again, and again. It's that simple.

I used to live in disaster-dieting mode. If I ate a piece of chocolate, candy or other sugary product, I thought my entire day or week or month was ruined! Today, I know that's not true. I just keep moving forward and make a better choice at the very next meal. Beating myself up about poor choices would inevitably lead me down the path of self-loathing and I would wind up eating junk food the entire day, or the entire week, for feeling like a failure.

One poorly chosen meal won't ruin my life, and it won't ruin yours either. It's not what I do once in a while that hurts my body - it's what I do daily. The key is to keep moving forward, no matter what, and make the next choice better than the last.

If I could change from a Standard American, junk food eater, alcohol, drug and cigarette abuser, coffee addict, dis-eased, and unhealthy person (whew, that was a mouthful!), then *you* can do it too.

Don't wait for a sickness to come to you. Strengthen your body right now and keep illness at bay. Insure your health today by consistently making better food and lifestyle choices.

Commit to reclaiming your health and start creating a better life as soon as possible. You are worth it! You can do it! Don't let anyone ever convince you otherwise, or suggest that you can't.

Mario Andretti said: "Desire is the key to motivation, but it's the determination and commitment to an unrelenting pursuit of your goal - a commitment to excellence - that will enable you to attain the success you seek."

By reading this book you have proven that you already have the "desire" and the "motivation" to transition your health. Now... don't be afraid to make some significant commitments to *you* and your health-related goals, and create a successful lifetime of wellness. The pages that follow will guide you.

HEALTH RELATED GOALS

Make a list of health related goals you would like to achieve. Writing your goals gives it more weight – ink weight that is! You could pick one main goal or as many as you'd like. The key is not to overwhelm your self with too much to do at once. Take it easy. One day at a time, one step at a time, one meal at a time. After you've written your goals turn to the following page and make some commitments to help you reach them.

Examples:

- Reach my ideal weight
- Heal an illness
- Look and feel my absolute best

- _____

- _____

- _____

COMMITMENTS

I _____(your name)

commit to create a lifetime of wellness by taking the following actions to

reach my goals:

Examples:

- Eat organic food as often as possible
- Take a daily walk
- Breathe deeply

- _____

- _____

- _____

- _____

- _____

- _____

As mentioned, if you break commitments to your self and your goals do NOT beat yourself up about it. Just re-commit and try to make a better choice next time. The main key is to keep showing up for yourself and move forward, no matter what, because you are worth it.

You are worth every single positive action you can do for yourself, no matter how big or small. The more you consistently and consciously care for yourself, the more it will increase your self-love. And, here's the kicker… the more you *love* yourself, the easier it is to take care of yourself. It's a nice catch twenty-two.

With that being said… love yourself, be good to yourself, and make the best choices as often as possible.

Aristotle wrote: "We are what we repeatedly do. Excellence then, is not an act, but a habit."

You can create excellent health-promoting habits over time, with patience, love and persistence. Now get started and reclaim your health today!

Check out other great products at http://www.AndreaBeaman.com

Now that you are inspired to reclaim your health, the next step is to get better quality food into your life and make it taste absolutely delicious. **The Whole Truth Eating and Recipe Guide** has over 100 mouthwatering recipes to make better food and better health a reality for you!

Personal Coaching with Andrea Beaman

Andrea Beaman is a certified Holistic Health Counselor and Food Expert with the experience to guide you to greater health and wellness.

She dramatically improved her own health by eating better quality foods and living more successfully. She will share these valuable insights with you, one to one via phone, email or in person, to help you get better foods and lifestyle improvements into your life.

Andrea will inspire, educate and support you as you transition from nutrient poor foods and grow beyond old eating patterns.

Lifestyle changes are made simple. She'll work with you to develop a step-by-step plan to realize dramatically improved health, greater enjoyment from eating, and the confidence that comes from knowing how.

With a personalized solution, you can join countless others as you reclaim your health, achieve your ideal weight, increase energy, and look and feel your best.

Get the guidance and ongoing support you may need, to succeed.

1. Go to http://www.AndreaBeaman.com
2. Click on Products and Services
3. Sign up for 1 month, 3 months or 6 months

Mention you read The Whole Truth, and you'll receive a special bonus worth **$150**

Printed in the United States
74024LV00003B/1-66

9 780977 869305